THE ART OF
WORLDLY WISDOM

By BALTASAR GRACIÁN

Translated by JOSEPH JACOBS

The Art of Worldly Wisdom
By Baltasar Gracián
Translated by Joseph Jacobs

Print ISBN 13: 978-1-4209-6095-2
eBook ISBN 13: 978-1-4209-6014-3

Cover Image: a detail of "A Vanitas Still Life of Musical Instruments and Manuscripts, an Overturned Gilt Covered Goblet, a Jewellery Casket, a Candlestick, an Astrological Globe, a String of Pearls, Jewels, Shells, a Skull and Femur and an Hour-Glass on a Draped Table", c. 1653 (oil on canvas), by Pieter Claesz (1597-1660) / Private Collection / Photo © Christie's Images / Bridgeman Images.

Please visit *www.digireads.com*

CONTENTS

Auf des Glückes großer Waage
Steht die Zunge selten ein;
Du mußt steigen oder sinken,
Du mußt herrschen und gewinnen,
Oder dienen und verlieren,
Leiden oder triumphieren,
Amboß oder Hammer sein.

GOETHE, *Ein Kophtisches Lied.*

When you are an anvil, hold you still,
When you are a hammer, strike your fill.

G. HERBERT, *Jacula Prudentum.*

To Mrs. G. H. Lewis

Dear Mrs. Lewis,

This little book were not worthy of being associated with your name, did it not offer an ideal of life at once refined and practical, cultured yet wisely energetic. Gracian points to noble aims, and proposes, on the whole, no ignoble means of attaining to them. The Spanish Jesuit sees clear, but he looks upward.

There is, however, one side of life to which he is entirely blind, as was perhaps natural in an ecclesiastic writing before the Age of Salons. He nowhere makes mention in his pages of the gracious influence of Woman as Inspirer and Consoler in the Battle of Life. Permit me to repair this omission by placing your name in the forefront of this English version of his maxims. To those honored with your friendship this will by itself suffice to recall all the ennobling associations connected with your sex.

Believe me, dear Mrs. Lewis,
Yours most sincerely,
JOSEPH JACOBS.

KILBURN, *26th October* 1892.

Preface

My attention was first drawn to the *Oráculo Manual* by Mr. (now Sir Mountstuart) Grant Duff's admirable article on Balthasar Gracian in the *Fortnightly Review* of March 1877. I soon after obtained a copy of Schopenhauer's excellent version, and during a journey in Spain I procured with some difficulty a villainously printed edition of Gracian's works (Barcelona, 1734, "Por Joseph Giralt"), which contains the *Oráculo Manual* towards the end of the first volume (pp. 431-494).

I have translated from this last, referring in the many doubtful places of its text to the first Madrid edition of 1653, the earliest in the British Museum. I have throughout had Schopenhauer's version by my side, and have found it, as Sir Mountstuart Grant Duff says, "a most finished piece of work," though I have pointed out in the Notes a few cases where he has failed, in my opinion, to give Gracian's meaning completely or correctly. I have little doubt that I am a fellow-sinner in this regard: I know no prose style that offers such difficulty to a translator as Gracian's laconic and artificial epigrams. It is not without reason that he has been called the Intraducible. The two earlier English versions miss his points time after time, and I found it useless to refer to them. On the other hand, I have ventured to adopt some of Sir Mountstuart Grant Duff's often very happy renderings in the extracts contained in his *Fortnightly* article.

I have endeavored to reproduce Gracian's Laconism and *Cultismo* in my version, and have even tried to retain his many paronomasias and jingles of similar sound. I may have here and there introduced others of my own to redress the balance for cases where I found it impossible to produce the same effect in English. In such cases I generally give the original in the Notes. Wherever possible I have replaced Spanish proverbs and proverbial phrases by English ones, and have throughout tried to preserve the characteristic rhythm and brevity of the Proverb. In short, if I may venture to say so, I have approached my task rather in the spirit of Fitzgerald than of Bohn.

The gem on the title, representing a votive offering to Hermes, the god of Worldly Wisdom, is from a fine paste in the British Museum of the best period of Greek glyptic art. I have to thank Mr. Cecil Smith of that Institution for kind advice in the selection.

Let me conclude these prefatory words with a piece of advice as oracular as my original: When reading this little book for the first time, read only fifty maxims and then stop for the day.

JOSEPH JACOBS.

Testimonia

Il est si concis si rompu et si estrangement coupé qu'il semble qu'il ait pris l'obscurité à tasche: aussi le Lecteur a besoin d'en deuiner le sens & souvent quand il l'a compris il trouve qu'il s'est estudié à faire une énigme d'une chose fort commune.

F. Van Aerssens, *Voyage d'Espagne*, 1667, p. 294.

Il a beaucoup d'élévation, de subtilité, de force et même de bon sens: mais on ne sait le plus souvent ce qu'il veut dire, et il ne le sait pas peut-être lui-même. Quelques-uns de ses Ouvrages ne semblent être fait, que pour n'être point entendus.

Bouhour's *Entretiens d'Ariste et d'Eugène*, 1671, p. 203.

Luisa de Padilla, a Lady of great Learning, and Countess of *Aranda*, was in like manner angry with the famous Gratian upon his publishing his Treatise of the *Discreto*, wherein she fancied that he had laid open those Maxims to common Readers, which ought only to be reserved for the knowledge of the Great. These Objections are thought by many of so much weight that they often defend the above-mention'd Authors by affirming they have affected such an Obscurity in their Style and Manner of Writing, that tho' every one may read their Works there will be but very few who can comprehend their Meaning.

The Spectator, No. 379 (1712).

En cherchant toujours l'énergie et le sublime il devient outré et se perd dans les mots. Gracian est aux bons moralistes ce que Don Quichotte est aux vrais héros. Its ont l'un et l'autre un faux air de grandeur qui en impose aux sots et qui fait rire les sages.

Abbe Desfontaines, 1745.

Qué de elogios no se deben al autor del *Criticon*! En medio de las antitesis, paronomasias y toda la metralla culta es una de las obras más recomendables de nuestra literatura por la felicidad de la invention, la inagotable riqueza de imagination y de sales, por la viveza de sus pinturas y por la gracia, soltura y naturalidad del estilo.

Don Manuel Sievela, *Biblioteca selecta de literatura española* (1819).

Si hubiese Gracian procedido con más sobriedad en el uso de estos juegos y conceptos ¿qual es el escritor de su tiempo de tantos dotes y caudal nativo para ser el más fecondo y elezante, sabiendo, como lo manifesto, en dónde estaban las delicadezas y los donaires, esto es, lo amargo, lo dulce, lo picante, lo salado de la lengua castellana?

Don Antonio Capmany, *Teatro de la elocuencia española*, tomo v.

The *Oráculo Manual* has been more used than any other of the author's works. It is intended to be a collection of maxims of general utility, but it exhibits good and bad precepts, sound judgments, and refined sophisms, all confounded together. In this work Gracian has not forgotten to inculcate his practical principles of Jesuitism to be all things to all men ("hacerse a todos"), nor to recommend his favorite maxim, "to be common in nothing" ("en nada vulgar"), which, in order to be valid, would require a totally different interpretation from that which he has given it.

Bouterwek.

The person, however, who settled the character of *cultismo* and in some respects gave it an air of philosophical pretension, was Baltazar Gracian, a Jesuit of Aragon, who lived between 1601 and 1658, exactly the period when the cultivated style took possession of Spanish prose and rose to its greatest consideration.

G. Ticknor, *History of Span. Lit.* iii. 222.

Dabei ist es das Einzige seiner Art und nie ein anderes über denselben Gegenstand geschrieben worden; denn nur ein Individuum aus der feinsten aller Nationen, der spanischen, konnte es versuchen. . . . Dasselbe lehrt die Kunst derer Allesich befliessigen und ist daher für Jedermann. Besonders aber ist es geeignet das Handbuch aller derer zu werden, die in der grossen Welt leben, ganz vorzüglich aber junger Leute, die ihr Glück darin zu machen bemüht sind und denen es mit Einem Mal und zum Voraus die Belehrung giebt die sie sonst erst durch lange Erfahrung erhalten.

A. Schopenhauer, *Litterarische Notiz we seiner Uebersetzung* (1831, published 1861).

Avec beaucoup d'esprit, d'instruction & de facilité il n'a rien produit qui puisse aujourd'hui soutenir l'examen de la critique la plus impartiale.

Puibusque, *Histoire comparée des littératures espagnole et française*, 1843, i. p. 559.

Gracian aurait pu être un excellent écrivain s'il n'avait pas voulu devenir un écrivain extraordinaire. Doué d'une vaste érudition, d'un esprit fin, d'un talent profond d'observation, il était né pour éclairer son siècle; mais la vanité de devenir novateur corrompit son gout, en le portant à introduire dans la prose ce langage précieux, ces expressions alambiquées que Gongora avait introduit dans les vers.

A. DE BACKER, *Bibliothèque des écrivains de la Compagnie de Jésus*, 1869, *s.v.* Gracian.

Asi como las máximas de Antonio Perez fueron muy populares entre cortesanos ó doctos ó ilustrados, así españoles como extranjeros, por aquella delicadeza especial de estilo, las del Padre Baltasar Gracian alcanzaron la misma estima por ese atildamiento en el decir: atildamiento que tenia en si un inexplicable atractivo, y que aunque algo participaba del general culteranismo de la literatura española en aquel siglo, encerraba cierto buen gusto deslumbrador y lisonjero para el lector que on profundisimos conceptos preciaba con la fuerza de su ingenio aquellos.

DON ADOLFO DE CASTRO, *Obras escogidas de Filósofia*, 1873, p. cviii.

Taking the book as a guide, especially for those who intend to enter public life, I have never chanced to meet with anything which seemed to me even distantly to approach it . . . It would possibly be rather difficult to disprove the thesis that the Spanish nation has produced the best maxims of practical wisdom, the best proverb, the best epitaph, and the best motto in the world, If I had to sustain it, I would point with reference to the first head to the *Oráculo Manual*.

Sir M. E. GRANT DUFF on "Balthasar Gracian" in *Fortnightly Review*, March 1877.

Some have found light in the sayings of Balthasar Gracian, a Spaniard who flourished at the end of the seventeenth century. . . . I do not myself find Gracian much of a companion, though some of his aphorisms give a neat turn to a commonplace.

J. MORLEY on "Aphorisms," *Studies*, 1891, p. 86.

Introduction

I. Of Balthasar Gracian and his Works

We may certainly say of Gracian what Heine by an amiable fiction said of himself: he was one of the first men of his century. For he was born 8th January 1601 N.S.[1] at Belmonte, a suburb of Calatayud, in the kingdom of Aragon. Calatayud, properly Kalat Ayoub, "Job's Town," is nearly on the site of the ancient Bilbilis, Martial's birthplace. As its name indicates, it was one of the Moorish settlements, and nearly one

---

[1] The ordinary authorities vary between 1594 and 1604. I follow Latassa y Ortin, *Biblioteca nueva de los escritores Aragoneses*, Pamplona, 1799, iii. 267 *seq.*, practically the only original source for Gracian's life and works.

of the most northern. By Gracian's time it had again been Christian and
Spanish for many generations, and Gracian himself was of noble birth.
For a Spaniard of noble birth only two careers were open, arms and the
Church. In the seventeenth century arms had yielded to the cassock,
and Balthasar and his three brothers all took orders. Felipe, his eldest,
joined the order of St. Francis; the next brother, Pedro, became a
Trinitarian during his short life; and the third, Raymundo, became a
Carmelite.[2] Balthasar himself tells us (*Agudeza*, c. xxv.) that he was
brought up in the house of his uncle, the licentiate Antonio Gracian, at
Toledo, from which we may gather that both his father and his mother,
a Morales, died in his early youth. He joined the Company of Jesus in
1619, when in its most flourishing state, after the organizing genius of
Acquaviva had given solid form to the bold counter-stroke of Loyola to
the Protestant Revolution. The *Ratio Studiorum* was just coming into
full force, and Gracian was one of the earliest men in Europe to be
educated on the system which has dominated the secondary education
of Europe almost down to our own days. This point is of some
importance, we shall see, in considering Gracian's chief work.

Once enrolled among the ranks of the Jesuits, the individual
disappears, the Jesuit alone remains. There is scarcely anything to
record of Gracian's life except that he was a Jesuit, and engaged in
teaching what passes with the Order for philosophy and sacred
literature, and became ultimately Rector of the Jesuit College at
Tarragona. His great friend was Don Vincencio Juan de Lastanosa, a
dilettante of the period, who lived at Huesca, and collected coins,
medals, and other archæological bric-a-brac. Gracian appears to have
shared his tastes, for Lastanosa mentions him in his description, of his
own cabinet. A long correspondence with him was once extant and
seen by Latassa, who gives the dates and places where the letters were
written. From these it would seem that Gracian moved about
considerably from Madrid to Zarogoza, and thence to Tarragona. From
another source we learn that Philip III. often had him to dinner to
provide Attic salt to the royal table. He preached, and his sermons were
popular. In short, a life of prudent prosperity came to an end when
Balthasar Gracian, Rector of the Jesuit College at Tarragona, died there
6th December 1658, at the age of nearly fifty-eight years.

Of Gracian's works there is perhaps more to say even while
leaving for separate consideration that one which is here presented to
the English reader and forms his chief claim to attention. Spanish
literature was passing into its period of swagger, a period that came to
all literatures of modern Europe after the training in classics had given
afresh the sense of style. The characteristic of this period in a literature
is suitably enough the appearance of "conceits" or elaborate and far-

---

[2] Gracian mentions his brothers in his *Agudeza*.

fetched figures of speech. The process began with Antonia Guevara, author of *El Libro Aureo*, from which, according to some, the English form of the disease known as Euphuism was derived. But it received a further impetus from the success of the *stilo culto* of Gongora in poetry.[3] Gongorism drove "conceit" to its farthest point: artificiality of diction could go no farther in verse: it was only left for Gracian to apply it to prose.

He did this for the first time in 1630 in his first work, *El Heroe*. This was published, like most of his other works, by his lifelong friend Lastanosa, and under the name of Lorenzo Gracian, a supposititious brother of Gracian's, who, so far as can be ascertained, never existed. The whole of *El Heroe* exists, in shortened form, in the *Oráculo Manual*.[4] The form, however, is so shortened that it would be difficult to recognize the original *primores*, as they are called, of *El Heroe*. Yet it is precisely in the curtness of the sentences that the peculiarity of the stilo culto consists. Generally elaborate metaphor and far-fetched allusions go with long and involved sentences of the periodic type. But with Gracian the aim is as much towards shortness as towards elaboration. The embroidery is rich but the jacket is short, as he himself might have said. As for the subject-matter, the extracts in the *Oráculo* will suffice to give some notion of the lofty ideal or character presented in *El Heroe*, the ideal indeed associated in the popular mind with the term hidalgo.[5]

A later book, *El Discreto*, first published in 1647, gives the counterpoise to *El Heroe* by drawing an ideal of the prudent courtier as contrasted with the proud and spotless hidalgo. This too is fully represented in the book before us, but the curtailment is still more marked than in the case of *El Heroe*. There is evidence that Gracian wrote a similar pair of contrasts, termed respectively *El Galante* and *El Varon Atento*, which were not published but were incorporated in the Oráculo Manual by Lastanosa. The consequences of this utilization of contrasts will concern us later.

Reverting to Gracian's works somewhat more in their order, his *éloge* of Ferdinand, the Magus of Columbus' epoch, need not much detain us. It is stilted and conventional and does not betray much historical insight. Gracian's *Agudeza y Arte de Ingenio* is of more importance and interest as the formal exposition of the critical principles of *Cultismo*. It is concerned more with verse than prose and

---

[3] On Gongora and his relation to *Cultismo* see Ticknor, *Hist. Span. Lit.* iii. 18 seq.; also Appendix G, "On the origin of Cultismo." Ticknor is, however, somewhat prejudiced against any form of *Cultismo*.

[4] See Notes to Maxims xxvi, xxxviii, xl, xlii, xliv, xl, lxiii, lxv, lxvii, xciv, xcviii, cvi, cxxvii.

[5] See Notes to Maxims ii, xx, xxii, xxv, xlix, li, liii, lv, lvi, lix, lxix, lxxi, lxxvi, lxxxvii, cxxii, cxxvii, cclxxvii, ccxcv.

represents the *Poetics* of Gongorism. A curious collection of flowers of rhetoric in Spanish verse could be made from it. Of still more restricted interest is the *Comulgador* or sacred meditations for holy communion. I do not profess to be a judge of this class of literature, if literature it can be called, but the fact that the book was deemed worthy of an English translation as lately as 1876 seems to show that it still answers the devotional needs of Catholics. It has a personal interest for Gracian, as it was the only book of his that appeared under his own name.

There remains only to be considered, besides the Oráculo Manual, Gracian's *El Criticon*, a work of considerable value and at least historic interest which appeared in the three parts dealing with Youth, Maturity, and Old Age respectively during the years 1650-53. This is a kind of philosophic romance or allegory depicting the education of the human soul. A Spaniard named Critilo is wrecked on St: Helena, and there finds a sort of Man Friday,[6] whom he calls Andrenio. Andrenio, after learning to communicate with Critilo, gives him a highly elaborate autobiography of his soul from the age of three days or so. They then travel to Spain, where they meet Truth, Valor, Falsehood, and other allegorical females and males, who are labeled by Critilo for Andrenio's benefit in the approved and frigid style of the allegorical teacher. Incidentally, however, the ideals and aspirations of the Spaniard of the seventeenth century are brought out, and from this point of view the book derives the parallel with the *Pilgrim's Progress* which Ticknor had made for it.[7] It is certainly one of the most characteristic products of Spanish literature, both for style and subject-matter.

Nearly all these works of Gracian were translated into most of the cultured languages of Europe, English not excepted.[8] Part of this ecumenical fame was doubtless due to the fact that Gracian was a Jesuit, and brethren of his Order translated the works of one of whom the Order was justly proud. But this explanation cannot altogether account for the wide spread of Gracian's works, and there remains a deposit of genuine ability and literary skill involved in most of the works I have briefly referred to—ability and skill of an entirely obsolete kind nowadays, but holding a rank of their own in the seventeenth and eighteenth centuries, when didacticism was all the rage. It is noteworthy that the *Testimonia* I have collected for the most part pass over the *Oráculo*, the only work at which a modern would care to cast a second glance, and go into raptures over *El Criticon* and

---

[6] It is not impossible that the English translation of *The Critick* by Rycaut, 1681, may have suggested the Friday incidents of *Robinson Crusoe*, which was intended to be a more didactic book than it looks.

[7] Ticknor also suggests that the *Criticon* was derived from the *Euphormion* of Barclay, the author of *Argenis*.

[8] See the details in the Bibliographical Appendix to this Introduction.

its fellows, or the reverse of raptures on Gracian's style, which after all was the most striking thing about his works.

That style reaches its greatest perfection in the *Oráculo Manual*, to which we might at once turn but for a preliminary inquiry which it seems worthwhile to make. It is a book of maxims as distinguished from a book of aphorisms, and it is worthwhile for several reasons inquiring into maxims in general and maxim literature in particular before dealing with what is probably the most remarkable specimen of its class.

Before, however, doing this we may close this section of our introductory remarks by "putting in," as the lawyers say, the Latin inscription given by Latassa from the foot of the portrait of Gracian, which once stood in the Jesuit College at Calatayud, a portrait of which, alas! no trace can now be found. The lines sum up in sufficiently forcible Latin all that need be known of Balthasar Gracian and his works.

P. BALTHASAR GRACIAN VT IAM AB ORTV EMINERET
IN BELLOMONTE NATVS EST PROPE BILBILIM
CONFINIS MARTIALIS PATRIA PROXIMVS INGENIO,
VT PROFVNDERET ADHVC CHRISTIANAS ARGVTIAS
    BILBILIS
QVÆ PŒNE EXHAVSTA VIDEBATVR IN ETHNICIS.
ERGO AVGENS NATALE INGENIVM INNATO ACVMINE
    SCRIPSIT
ARTEM INGENII ET ARTE FACIT SCIBILE QVOD SCIBILES
    FACIT ARTES.
SCRIPSIT ITEM ARTEM PRVDENTIAE ET A SE IPSO ARTEM
    DIDICIT.
SCRIPSIT ORACVLVM ET VOCES SVAS PROTVLIT.
SCRIPSIT DISERTVM VT SE IPSVM DESCRIBERET
ET VT SCRIBERET HEROEM HEROICA PATRAVIT.
HÆC ET ALIA EIVS SCRIPTA MOECENATES REGES
    HABVERVNT
IVDICES ADMIRATIONEM LECTOREM MVNDVM
TYPOGRAPHVM ÆTERNITATEM. PHILIPPVS III. SÆPE ILLIVS
    ARGVTIAS
INTER PRANDIVM VERSABAT NE DEFICERENT SALES
REGIIS DAPIBVS. SED QVI PLAVSVS EXCITAVERAT
CALAMO DEDITVS MISSIONIBVS EXCITAVIT PLANCTVS
    VERBO
EXCITATVRVS DESIDERIVM IN MORTE QVA RAPTVS FVIT
VI. DECEMBRIS AN. MDCLVIII SED ALIQVANDO EXTINCTVS
    ÆTERNVM LVCEBIT.

II. Of Maxims

Many men have sought to give their views about man and about life in a pithy way; a few have tried to advise men in short sentences what to do in the various emergencies of life. The former have written aphorisms, the latter maxims. Where the aphorism states a fact of human nature, a maxim advises a certain course of action. The aphorism is written in the indicative, the maxim in an imperative mood.[9] "Life is interesting if not happy," is an aphorism, of Professor Seely's, I believe. "Ascend a step to choose a friend, descend a step to choose a wife," is a maxim of Rabbi Meir, one of the Doctors of the Talmud.

Now it is indeed curious how few maxims have ever been written. Wisdom has been extolled on the house-tops, but her practical advice seems to have been kept secret. Taking our own literature, there are extremely few books of practical maxims, and not a single one of any great merit. Sir Walter Raleigh's *Cabinet Council*, Penn's *Maxims*, and Chesterfield's *Letters* almost exhaust the list, and the last generally contains much more than mere maxims. Nor are they scattered with any profusion through books teeming with knowledge of life, the galaxy of English novels. During recent years extracts of their "beauties" have been published in some profusion—*Wit and Wisdom of Beaconsfield*; *Wise, Witty, and Tender Sayings of George Eliot*; *Extracts from Thackeray*, and the rest—but the crop of practical maxims to be found among them is extremely scanty. Aphorisms there are in plenty, especially in George Eliot, but he that is doubtful what course to pursue in any weighty crisis would woefully waste his time if he sought for advice from the novelists.

Nor are the moralists more instructive in this regard. Bacon's *Essays* leave with one the impression of fullness of practical wisdom. Yet, closely examined, there is very little residue of practical advice left in his pregnant sayings. Even the source of most of this kind of writing, the Biblical book of Proverbs, fails to answer the particular kind of test I am at present applying. However shrewd some of them are, startling us with the consciousness how little human nature has changed, it is knowledge of human nature that they mainly supply. When we ask for instruction how to apply that knowledge we only get variations of the theme "Fear the Lord." Two thousand years of experience have indeed shown that the Fear or Love of the Lord forms a very good foundation for practical wisdom. But it has to be supplemented by some such corollary as "Keep your powder dry" before it becomes of direct service in the conduct of life.

---

[9] Not to be misleading, I may mention that Gracian's are generally in the infinitive.

It is indeed because of the unpractical nature of practical maxims that they have been so much neglected. You must act in the concrete, you can only maximize in general terms. Then, again, maxims can only appeal to the mind, to the intellect: the motive force of action is the will, the temperament. As Disraeli put it: "The conduct of men depends on the temperament, not upon a bunch of musty maxims" (*Henrietta Temple*). It is only very distantly that a maxim can stir the vague desire that spurs an imitative will. True, at times we read of men whose whole life has been colored by a single saying. But these have generally been more appeals to the imagination, like Newman's "Securus judicat orbis terrarum," or the "Heu! fuge crudeles terras, fuge litus avarum," which had so decisive an effort on Savonarola's life. It is rare indeed that a man's whole life is tinged by a single practical maxim like Sir Daniel Gooch, who was influenced by his father's advice, "Stick to one thing."

Perhaps one of the reasons that have led literary persons to neglect the Maxim as a literary form has been their own ignorance of Action and, still more, their exaggerated notions of its difficulties and complexities. Affairs are not conducted by aphorisms: war is waged by a different kind of Maxims from those we are considering. Yet after all there must be some general principles on which actions should be conducted, and one would think they could be determined. Probably the successful men of action are not sufficiently self-observant to know exactly on what their success depends, and, if they did, they would in most cases try to "keep it in the family," like their wealth or their trade secrets.

And perhaps after all they are right who declare that action has little to do with intellect, and much with character. To say the truth, one is not impressed with the intellectual powers of the millionaires one meets. The shadiest of journalists could often explain their own doings with more point than they. Yet there are surely intellectual qualifications required for affairs: the Suez Canal must have required as great an amount of research, emendation, sense of order, and organization as, say, the *Corpus Inscriptionum Latinarum*. But there is no such punishment for slovenly scholarship in action as there is in letters. The Suez Canal can be dug only once: Lucretius or Latin inscriptions can be edited over and over again. Altogether we need not be surprised if the men of action cannot put the principles of action into pointed sentences or maxims.

And if men of action cannot, it is not surprising that men of letters do not. For they cannot have the interest in action and its rewards which is required for worldly success, or else they would not be able to concentrate their thoughts on things which they consider of higher import. To a man of letters the world is the devil, or ought to he if he is to have the touch of idealism which gives color and weight to his words. How then is he to devote his attention to worldly wisdom and the maxims that are to teach it? It is characteristic in this connection that the weightiest writer of maxims in our language is Bacon, who attempted to combine a career of affairs and of thought, and spoilt both by so doing.

It is perhaps due to the subtle and all-embracing influence of Christianity on modern civilization that this divorce between idealism and the world has come about. The strenuous opposition to the world among earnest Christians has led to their practical withdrawal from it. Just as the celibacy of the clergy meant that the next generation was to be deprived of the hereditary influence of some of the purest spirits of the time, so the opposition of Christianity to the world has brought it about that the world has been un-Christian. Only one serious attempt has been made to bridge the chasm. The *idée mère* of Jesuitism was to make the world Christian by Christians becoming worldly. It was doubtless due to the reaction against the over-spiritualization of Christianity pressed by the Protestant Reformation, but its practical result has been to make the Jesuit a worldly Christian. The control of the higher education of Europe by the Jesuits has tended, on the other hand, to make society more Christian. If then we were to look for an adequate presentation of worldly wisdom touched with sufficient idealism to make it worthy of a man of letters, we should look for it from a Jesuit, or from one trained among the Jesuits.

After all this elaborate explanation why so few maxims have been composed it may seem contradictory to give as a further and final reason because so many exist—under another form. For what are the majority of proverbs but maxims under another name, or rather maxims without the name of their author? We say of proverbs, indeed, that they arise among the people, but it is one definite individual among the people that gives them the piquant form that makes them proverbial. It was, we may be sure, a definite English gaffer who first said, "Penny wise, pound foolish." If we knew his name, we should call it maxim; as his name is unknown it ranks as a proverb. In this connection the Talmudic proverbs and maxims are of great interest. Owing to the worthy Rabbinic principle, "Say a thing in the name of the man who said it," we can in almost all cases trace Talmudic proverbs to their authors; or, in other words, Talmudic proverbs remain maxims. There is only one analogous case in English; a few of Benjamin Franklin's maxims, *e.g.* "Three removes are as good as a fire,"[10] have become proverbs.

The abundance of proverbs is extraordinary. There is a whole bibliography devoted to the literature of proverbs (Duplessis, *Bibliographie Parémiologique*, Paris, 1847), and this needs nowadays a

---

[10] Most persons have heard the cynical continuation of a modern: "Three fires are as good as a failure and three failures are as good as a fortune."

supplement as large again as the original (partly supplied by the bibliographical Appendix of Haller, *Altspanische Sprichwörter*, 1883). Indeed in the multitude of proverbs consists the greatest proof of their uselessness as guides to action, for by this means we get proverbs at cross purposes. Thus take the one I have just referred to, "Penny wise, pound foolish," which has a variant in the proverb, "Do not spoil the ship for a ha'porth of tar." A man who was hesitating as to the amount or expense he would incur in any undertaking would be prompted by these sayings to be lavish. But then how about the proverb, "Take care of the pence and the pounds will take care of themselves"? Between the two proverbs he would come to the ground, and if he has the νους to decide between them, he does not need the proverbs at all.

Hence it is perhaps that the nation that is richest in proverbs is the one that has proved itself among European peoples the least wise in action. To the Spaniards has been well applied the witticism about Charles II.: "They never said a foolish thing and never did a wise one." Certainly if proverbs be a proof of wisdom the Spaniards have given proofs in abundance. *Don Quixote* is full of them and the Spanish collections are extraordinarily rich. Now the nation that can produce good proverbs should be able to produce good maxims; hence we should expect the best book of maxims to emanate from a Spaniard.

One characteristic of both these forms of practical wisdom is their artificiality. One has to think twice before the point of a proverb or a maxim is perfectly clear. "The early bird catches the worm" seems at first sight as meaningless a proposition as "There are milestones on the Dover Road." Hence it is when a literature is passing through its artificial stage that maxims would naturally appear. So that it was clearly preordained that when *the* book of maxims should appear it would be by a Jesuit, so as to be worldly yet not too worldly; by a Spaniard, so that it should have the proverbial ring; and during the prevalence of *cultismo*, so that it should have the quaintness to attract attention.

III. Of the "Oráculo Manual"

Having thus proved *à priori* that the ideal book of maxims was destined to be the *Oráculo Manual* of Balthasar Gracian, let us proceed to prove our proof, as schoolboys do with their sums. That it is the best book of maxims is a foregone conclusion, because there is none other. Schopenhauer, who translated the book, observes that there is nothing like it in German, and there is certainly none approaching it in English, and if France or Italy can produce its superior, it is strange that its fame has remained so confined to its native country.

Not that there are not books teaching the art of self-advancement in almost all languages. The success of Dr. Smiles's volume on Self-Help is a sufficient instance of this.[11] Curiously enough, Dr. Smiles's book has had its greatest success in Italy, where it has given rise to quite a *letteratura selfelpista*, as the Italians themselves call it. Or rather not curiously, for if you wish to find the most unromantic set of ideals nowadays you must go search among the Romance nations.

Gracian does not, however, compete with Dr. Smiles. He does not deal with *Brodweisheit*; he assumes that the vulgar question of bread and butter has been settled in favor of his reader. He may be worldly, but he is thinking of the great world. He writes for men with a position and how to make the most of it. Nor is the aim he puts before such persons an entirely selfish one. "The sole advantage of power is that you can do more good" is the only rational defense of ambition, and Gracian employs it (Max. cclxxxvi).

Indeed the tone of the book is exceptionally high. It is impossible to accuse a man of any meanness who is the author of such maxims as—

"One cannot praise a man too much who speaks well of them who speak ill of him" (clxii).

"Friends are a second existence" (cxi).

"When to change the conversation? When they talk scandal" (ccl).

"In great crises there is no better companion than a bold heart" (clxvii).

"The secret of long life: lead a good life" (xc).

"Be able to boast that if gallantry, generosity, and fidelity were lost in the world men would be able to find them again in your own breast" (clxv).

"A man of honor should never forget what he is because he sees what others are" (cclxxx).

And there are whole sections dealing with such topics as Rectitude (xxix), Sympathy with great Minds (xliv), a genial Disposition (lxxix), and the like.

Not that he is without the more subtle devices of the worldly wise. One could not wish to have anything more cynical or stinging than the following:—

"Find out each man's thumbscrew" (xxvi).

"A shrewd man knows that others when they seek him do not seek *him*, but their advantage in him and by him" (cclii).

"The truth, but not the whole truth" (clxxxi).

"Keep to yourself the final touches of your art" (ccxii).

"Do not take payment in politeness" (cxci).

"Have a touch of the trader" (ccxxxii).

"Think with the few and speak with the many" (xliii).

---

[11] One of our public men, I have been told, is known among his friends by the sobriquet of "Self-help by smiles."

"Never have a companion who casts you in the shade" (clii).

"Never become paradoxical in order to avoid the trite" (cxliii).[12]

"Do not show your wounded finger" (cxlv).

The characteristic of the book is this combination or rather contrast of high tone and shrewdness. Gracian is both wisely worldly and worldly wise. After all, there does not seem to be any inherent impossibility in the combination. There does not seem any radical necessity why a good man should be a fool. One always has a certain grudge against Thackeray for making his Colonel Newcome so silly at times, though perhaps the irony, the pathos, the tragedy of the book required it. As a matter of fact the holiest of men have been some of the shrewdest, for their friends at least, if not for themselves.

The explanation of the combination in Gracian is simple enough. He was a Jesuit, and the Jesuits have just that combination of high tone and worldly wisdom as their *raison d'être*. And in the case of the *Oráculo* the mixture was easily effected by Gracian or his friend Lastanosa. For Gracian had written at least two series of works in which this contrast was represented by separate books. Two of these describing the qualities of the Hero and the Prudent Man (*El Heroe* and *El Discreto*) were published and are represented in the *Oráculo*.[13] Two others dealing with the Gallant and the Cautious Man (*El Galante* and *El Varon Atento*) are referred to by Lastanosa in the preface to *El Discreto*, and are also doubtless represented in the book before us. One may guess that the section on Highmindedness (cxxviii) or on Nobility of Feeling (cxxxi) comes from *El Galante*, while "Better mad with the rest of the world than wise alone" (cxxxiii) smacks of *El Varon Atento*. At times we get the two tones curiously intermingled: "Choose an heroic ideal" (lxxv) seems at first sight a noble sentiment, but Gracian goes on to qualify it by adding, "but rather to emulate than to imitate."

The modernness of the tone is the thing that will strike most readers apart from these contrasts. Here and there one may be struck by an archaic note. "Never compete" would scarcely be the advice of a worldly teacher nowadays. But on the whole there is a tone of modern good society about the maxims which one would scarcely find in contemporary English works like Peacham's, or even in contemporary French authors like Charron. The reason is that modern society is permeated by influences which Gracian himself represented. The higher education of Europe for the last two and a half centuries has been in the hands of Jesuits or in schools formed on the *Ratio Studiorum*. And Society in the stricter sense traces from the Hôtel Rambouillet, where one-half the influence was Spanish. Gracian thus directly represents the tone of the two Societies which have set the tone

---

[12] Mr. Oscar Wilde's attention may be respectfully called to this maxim.

[13] See *supra*, p. xxi. and notes.

of our society of to-day, and it is no wonder therefore if he is modern.

Even in his style there is something of a modern epigrammatic ring. At times there is the euphuistic quaintness, *e.g.* "One must pass through the circumference of time before arriving at the centre of opportunity." But as a rule the terseness and point of the maxim approximate to the modern epigram. "El escusarse antes de ocasion es culparse "might be both the source and the model of *Qui s'excuse s'accuse*. The terseness is indeed excessive and carried to Tacitean extremes. "A poco saber camino real," "Ultima felicidad el filosofar," "Harto presto, si bien." Gracian jerks out four or five words where a popular preacher would preach a sermon. Yet I cannot agree with the writers who call him obscure. He is one of the writers that make you think before you grasp his meaning, but the meaning is there, and put plainly enough, only tersely and very often indirectly, after the manner of proverbs. There is indeed no doubt that he and his predecessors were influenced by the form of the Spanish proverb in drawing up aphorisms and maxims. I say predecessors, for aphorismic literature at any rate was no novelty in Spain. Among the long list of books on aphorisms possessed by the late Sir William Stirling-Maxwell, and still at Keir, there are fully a dozen Spanish ones who precede Gracian(Hernando Diaz, Lopez de Corelas, and Melchior de Santa Cruz are the most important, though the latter is more full of anecdotage). Among them is a book of *Aforismos* by Antonio Perez, whose *Relaciones* has been the chief means of blackening Philip II.'s character.[14] The former are undoubtedly of the same style as Gracian, and probably influenced him, though, as they are aphorisms and not maxims, I have not been able to quote parallels in the Notes. Thus "Una obra vale millares de graçias" (Perez, *Afor.* i. 198) has the same proverbial ring. It is curious to see Lytton's "The pen is mightier than the sword" anticipated by Perez' "La pluma corta mas que espadas afiladas" (*ibid.* 199), or Voltaire's "Speech was given us to conceal our thoughts" in Perez' "Las palabras, vestido de los conçeptos" (ii. 130). This last example has all Gracian's terseness, while Perez' "Amigos deste Siglo, rostros humanos, coraçones de fieras"[15] (ii. 71) has both terseness and cynicism. Certainly the only other work in Spanish or any other literature preceding Gracian on anything like the same lines is this book of *Aforismos* by Antonio Perez.

It is somewhat of a question, to my mind, how far Gracian was the author of the final form of the maxims as we have them in the *Oráculo.* Those taken from *El Heroe* and *El Discreto* differ from their originals with great advantage. They are terser, more to the point and less

---

[14] On Perez see Mr. Froude's paper in his *Spanish Story of the Armada.* Perez was over in England and was of the Sidney set.

[15] "Friends nowadays, human faces, hearts of brutes."

euphuistic. Now the Address to the Reader has all these qualities, and we may assume was written by its signatory, Don Vincencio de Lastanosa. It is just possible that we owe to him the extreme terseness and point of the majority of the maxims of the *Oráculo Manual*. It must not, however, be assumed that they are all as pointed and epigrammatic as those I have quoted. Gracian seems advisedly to have imbedded his jewels in a duller setting. At times he vies with the leaders of the great sect of the Platitudinarians, and he can be as banal as he is brilliant. Even as it is, his very brilliancy wearies, and after fifty maxims or so one longs for a more fruity wisdom, a more digressive discussion of life like those learned, wise, and witty essays of Mr. Stevenson, which may someday take higher rank as literature than even his novels.

Perhaps, after all, the weariness to which I refer may be due to the cautious tone of the book. To succeed one must be prudent;[16] that is the great moral of the book, and if so, does it seem worthwhile to succeed? If life is to be denuded of the aleatory element, is it worth living? Well, Gracian meets you when in that temper too. It is indeed remarkable how frequently he refers to luck; how you are to trust your luck, weigh your luck, follow your luck, know your unlucky days, and so forth. Is all this a confession that after all life is too complex a game for any rules to be of much use? Granted, but there is one thing certain about life, and that is put by Goethe in the lines which I, following Schopenhauer,[17] have placed at the head of my translation. One must be either hammer or anvil in this world, and too great an excess of idealism only means that the unideal people shall rule the world. To guard against both extremes we have the paradoxical advice I have heard attributed to Mr. Ruskin, "Fit yourself for the best society, and then—never enter it."

Whether any ideal person will learn to rule the world by studying Gracian's or anyone else's maxims is somewhat more doubtful, for reasons I have given above in discussing proverbs. The man who can act on maxims can act without them, and so does not need them. And there is the same amount of contradiction in maxims as in proverbs. Thus, to quote an example from the book before us, from Max. cxxxii it would seem best to keep back an intended gift: "long expected is highest prized"; whereas from Max. ccxxxvi we learn that "the promptness of the gift obliges the more strongly." Which maxim are we to act upon? That depends on circumstances, and the judgment that can decide on the circumstances can do without the maxims. I cannot therefore promise success in the world to whomsoever may read this book; otherwise I should perhaps not have published it.

---

[16] The second title of the book is *Arte de Prudencia*, which I have adopted as the main title of my version.

[17] Gracian was his favorite author; "Mein Gracian" he called him on one occasion (*Memorabilien*, p. 505).

But whether Gracian's maxims are true or useful scarcely affects their value. To the student of literature as such, the flimsiest sentiment or the merest paradox aptly put is worth the sublimest truth ill expressed. And there can be little doubt that Gracian puts his points well and vigorously. I cannot hope to have reproduced adequately all the vigor and force of his style, the subtlety of his distinctions, or the shrewdness of his mother-wit. But enough, I hope, has emerged during the process of translation to convince the reader that Gracian's *Oráculo Manual* has much wisdom in small compass and well put.

Bibliographical Appendix

The best bibliographical account of Gracian's works is that of Backer, *Bibliothèque des écrivains de la Compagnie de Jésus*, 1869, *sub voce*. I have shortened the descriptions of the translations, etc., of the other works of Gracian, adding a few items from the British Museum Catalogue and other sources. The *Oráculo Manual* I have treated separately and more fully.

A. GRACIAN'S WORKS.

1. El Heroe de Lorenço Gracian Infanzon. Dedicado al Rey N.S. En Huesca por Juan Noguès, 1637, 8vo.
    [Published by Don Vincencio Juan de Lastanosa. According to Latassa the first edition was published in Madrid, 1630. Other editions in Madrid, 1639 Barcelona, 1640; Amsterdam, 1659 (por Juan Blaeu); also in the Biblioteca de autores españoles, 1873, t. lxv.
    French translation (1) by Gervais, médecin du roy, Paris, 1645; reprinted Amsterdam, 1659; (2) by P. de Courbeville, Paris, 1725.
    English translation (1) by Sir J. Skeffington, Lond. 1652; (2) from Courbeville's by a "gentleman of Oxford," Lond. 1726.]
2. El politico Don Ferdinando el católico de Lorenzo Gracian. Al excelentísimo Señor Duque de Nochera. En Zaragoza, 1640, 12°.
    [Published by Lastanosa. Reprinted Zaragoza, 1641, 16°; Huesca, 1646, 12°, Amsterdam, 1659.
    French translation (1) by M. de S. (Silhouette, Chancellor of the Duc d'Orleans), Paris, 1720; reprinted 1730, and Amsterdam, 1731; (2) by P. de Courbeville, 1732, 120.
    German translation by D. G. von Lohenstein.]
3. Agudeza y Acte de Ingenio en que se explican todos los modos y diferencias de conceptos. Madrid, 1642, 8vo.
    [Also published by Lastanosa. Other editions at Huesca, 1646 and 1648 (the latter with Salinas' translation of Martial).

Italian translation by a Genoese who passed it off as his own (*Journ. des Savants*, 1696, p. 333).]

4. El Discreto. Dedicado al serenísimo Señor Don Baltasar Carlos de Austria. En Huesca por Juan Nogues, 1645, 8vo.

[Published by Lastanosa. Republished Barcelona, 1647, 180; Brussels, 1665, 120; Amsterdam, 1665, 12°; also in Biblioteca de autores españoles, 1873, t. lxv.

French translation by De Courbeville; 2nd ed. Rotterdam, 1729.

English, "The Compleat Gentleman," by T. Salkeld 2nd ed. London, 1730; 3rd, Dublin, 1760.

German, Der Vollkommene Menach. Augsburg, 1729, 8vo, from the French.

Italian, L'Uomo Universale. Venice, 1725, from the French.

Polish by Brzostowski. Wilna, 1762, from the French.]

5. El Criticon. Primera Parte en la Primavera de la Niñez y en el Estio de la Juventad. En Madrid, 1650, 8vo—Segunda Parte Juyziosa y cortesana Filosofia en el Otoño de la Varonil Edad. En Huesca, 1653, 8vo—Tercera Parte en el Invierno de la Vejez. En Huesca, 1653, 8vo.

[Reprinted Madrid, 1658, 8vo.

English, Pt. I., by P. Rycaut. Lond. 1681.

French translation by Maunony. Paris, 1696-1708, 12°. Reprinted at La Hague, 1708, 1723, 1734; Rouen, 1709; Geneva, 1725.

Italian, by G. P. Cattaneo. Venice, 1685, 1698, 1709, 1720, 1745.

Dutch, by M. Smallegange. 'S Gravenhage, 1691, 120.

German, by C. Gottschling. Frankfurt, 1710; Halle, 1721.]

6. Oráculo Manual. See *infra* B.

7. El Comulgador: varias meditaciones para . . . la sacrada communion. Madrid, 1655, 12°.

[Reprinted Zaragoza, 1655, 160; Amberes, 1725, 4to; Valencia, 1736, 12°; Madrid, 1757, 8vo, 1788, 16°, 1826, 8vo; Paris, 1840, 24°, 1851, 18°, 1854, 18°, 1857, 18°, 1860, 18°.

English translation by M. Monteiro, 1876, 8vo.

French, by Amelot de la Houssaie. Paris, 1693, 8vo.

Italian, by Castro and Inviziati.

German, anon. Frankfort, 1734, 8vo; reprinted Vienna, 1738; and Nuremberg, 1751, with Appendix by W. Reithmeier, 1847.

Latin, anon. Munster, 1750-52, 120.]

8. Obras de Lorenzo Gracian. Amberes, 1652, 4to.

Reprinted Madrid, 1664, 4to; Barcelona, 1667. p. l 4to; Amberes, 1669, 4to; Madrid, 1674, 4to; Barcelona, 1700, 4to (with four idylls *Selvas de año*); Amberes, 1702, 4to, 1723,

4to; Madrid, 1720, 4to; Barcelona, 1734, 4to, 1748, 4to, 1757, 4to; Madrid 1773, 4to all in two vols.

Latassa also mentions various poems and letters which are scattered about, some in MS. For *El Varon Atento* and *El Galante* see supra p. xxii.

B. ORÁCULO MANUAL.

Early Spanish Bibliography is in a very bad state. One difficulty is that each of the smaller kingdoms of Spain seems to have had the right to reprint books published in any other division. We find this difficulty with the *Editio Princeps* of the *Oráculo Manual*. Latassa states that it was first published in Huesca, Aragon, in 1647, "Por Juan Nogues" (like most of Gracian's works). No copy of this edition is known to exist in any of the great libraries of Spain or other parts of Europe, and the earliest known is that contained in the British Museum with the following title:—

Oracvlo / Manval y Arte / de Prvdencia / Sacada de los a / forismos que
   de discurren en / las obras de Lorenzo Gracian. / Publicala D. Vi
   / cencio Juan de Lastanosa. Y la dedica / al Excelentissimo /
   Señor D. Luis Mendez / de Haro. Con licencia. En Madrid por
   Maria de Oiñones ano de 1653. / [160 pp. in 24°.]

But in the Censor's licence to this there is a distinct reference to a previous edition with which it is said to correspond ["coresponde con el antes impresso . . . que otras vezes ha sido impresso "]. This confirms Latassa's date of 1647 for the ED. PR. But this makes it difficult to understand Lastanosa's reference to the twelve books of Gracian's, of which the *Oráculo* was the quintessence.

Four only had been published by that time, and the two unpublished would make up only half a dozen. We must therefore leave the date of the ED. PR. a variable between 1647 and 1653, to be fixed by the future Spanish Lowndes or Hazlitt.

The *Oráculo* was reprinted at Amsterdam 1659, and henceforth it appeared in all the editions of the *Obras*. It is curious that it has never been reprinted separately in modern times in Spain, and can only be obtained in *Biblioteca de autores españoles*, tomo lxv. It has, however, been a book more honored abroad than in its own country, as the following list of Translations, taken mainly from Grisebach and the British Museum Catalogue, will show

I. ITALIAN.

1. Oracolo manuale, e Arte di Prudenza / Cavata dagl' Aforismi, che si
   discorrono nell' Opre di Lorenzo Gratiano / Mandalo in Luce D.
   Vincenzo Giovanni de Lastanosa. Diretto alla Nobiltá Venetiana e

dedicato all' Illustr. & Eccellentiss. Sig. Leonardo Pesaro . . . In Venetia MDCLXXIX.

> [Republished Venice, 1708, 1718, 1790.]

2. Huomo di Corte nuovamente tradotto dall' Abbate Francesa Tosques. Roma, 1698.

> [From the French. Republished Venice, 1730; Naples, 1740, 1761.]

II. FRENCH.

1. L'homme de cour de Baltasar Gracian. Traduit & commenté par le Sieur Amelot de la Houssaie, cidevant Secrétaire de l'Ambassade de France à Venise. Paris, 1684.

> [Reprinted La Hague, 1692; Lyons, 1693; Rotterdam, 1716, 1728; also editions in Paris, 1691, 170Z, 1732, 1765, 1808.]

2. Maximes de Baltazar Gracien, traduites de l'Espagnol [par J. de Courbeville]. Paris, 1730.

III. ENGLISH.

1. The / Courtier's / Oracle; / or the / Art of Prudence / . . . Written originally in Spanish / And now done into English. London, 1694.

> [From the French of Amelot de la Houssaie.]

2. The Art of Prudence; or a Companion for a Man of Sense. Made English . . and illustrated with the Sieur Amelot de la Houssaie's notes, by Mr. Savage. London, 1702.

> [Two more editions, 1705, 1714. The hook was simply a revision of the earlier translation.]

IV. LATIN.

1. Balthas. Graciani, Hispani, Aulicus sive de prudentia civili et maxime aulica liber singularis olim hispanice conscriptus, postes et Gallice, Italice, Germanice editus, nunc ex Ameloti versione Latine redditus . . . Franc. Glarianus Meldenus, Constantiensis, recensuit, latine vertit . . . et notis illustravit. Accessit Joh. Gottl. Heineccii J.C. praefatio. Francofurti ad Viadrum MDCCXXXI.

> [A reprint at Vienna, 1750.]

2. Hominis Aulici notum Graciani oraculum prudentiae, depromptum in sententiarum politicarum centurias III . . . Latinorum lingua loquens per interpretem P. A. Ulrich. 1734.

V. HUNGARIAN.

1. Bölts és figyelmetes udvari ember. Irta Spányol nyelven Grátzian B. Forditotta Németbül Faludi F. . . . Posonyban, 1770, 1771.
2. Udvari Kátó Vagy is Grátzián B. nak Faludi F. által Magyarra forditatott CCC Makszimai . . . Györölt, 1790.
   [In verse.]

VI. POLISH.

Baltazar Gracyan doskonalacy dworskiego człowjeka przez 300 maxym . . . Krakow, 1802.
[By Count Sierakowski.]

VII. GERMAN.

1. L'Homme de cour Oder der heutige politische Welt- und Staats-Weife / fürgestellet von Balthasar Gracian, Hispanieren Und wegen seiner hohen Würde in unsre hochteutche Sprache übersetzet anitzo aus dem Original vermehret, und zum Undernmahl herausgegeben von Joh Leonhard Sauter, J. U. D. Franctfurth und Leipzig, 1687.
   [Pp. CXVIII, 775, 240.]
2. Balthasar Gracian's Homme de Cour, oder: Kluger Hof- und Weltmann, nach Mr. Amelot de la Houssaie seiner französischen Version, in's Teutsche übersetzet von Selintes [= C. Weissbach]. Nebst Herrn C. Thomasii judicio vom Gracian. Augsburg, 1711.
3. Balthasar Gracians Oracul; d. i. Regeln der Klugheit. Aus dem Spanischen von A. F. Müller. 2 Bände. Leipzig, 1715-1717.
   [Two thick volumes containing Spanish original, Germ. paraphrase, and elaborate notes. Went into a second edition in 1733.]
4. Uomo di corte oder fluger Hof- und Weltmann. Nach der Italienischen Uebersetzung ins Deutsche übersetzt [von Christoph Heinrich Freisleben]. Ultenburg, 1723.
   [With the Italian text.]
5. Die Kunst zu leben; vortressliche Regeln eines alten Weltmannes fürs menschliche leben. Nach Balthasar Gracian [von K. H. Heydenreich], Leipzig, 1786.
6. Der Mann von Welt, eingeweiht in die Geheimnisse der Lebensflugheit, ein nach Balthasar Gracian frei bearbeitetes vollständig hinterlassenes Manuscript [von K. H. Heydenreich], Leipzig, Martini, 1803.
   [Reprinted Reutlingen, 1804.]

7. Dos schwarze Buch oder Lehren der Lebensweisheit Gracian's . . . 1826.
8. Männerschule von B. Gracian. Aus dem Spanischen übersetzt von Fr. Kölle. Stuttgart, 1838.
9. Balthasar Gracian's Handorafel und Kunst der Weltlugheit, treu und forgfältig übersetzt von Arthur Schopenhauer. Nachgelassenes, Leipzig, 1861.
> [Edited by Frauenstadt; reprinted 1862, 1877. Another edition from the original MS. by Grisebach in the Reclam series, 1889.]

VIII. DUTCH.

De Konst der Wysheit getrokken ujt de Spaensche van Gracian en nu vertaalt door M. Smallegange In's Gravenhage, MDCXCVI.

Leading Maxims

i. Everything is at its Acme (*Todo está ya en su punto*)
ii. Character and Intellect (*Genio y ingenio*)
iii. Keep Matters for a Time in Suspense (*Llevar sus cosas con suspencion*)
iv. Knowledge and Courage (*El saber y el valor*)
v. Create a Feeling of Dependence (*Hazer depender*)
vi. A Man at his Highest Point (*Hombre en su pinto*)
vii. Avoid Victories over Superiors (*Escusar vitorias del patron*)
viii. To be without Passions (*Hombre inapasionable*)
ix. Avoid the Faults of your Nation (*Desmentir los achaques de su nation*)
x. Fortune and Fame (*Fortuna y Fama*)
xi. Cultivate those who can teach you (*Tratar con quien se pueda aprender*)
xii. Nature and Art (*Naturaleza y Arte*)
xiii. Act sometimes on Second Thoughts, sometimes on First Impulse (*Obrar de intencion, ya segunda y ya primera*)
xiv. The Thing Itself and the Way it is done (*La realidad ye el modo*)
xv. Keep Ministering Spirits (*Tener ingenios auxiliares*)
xvi. Knowledge and Good Intentions (*Saber con recta intention*)
xvii. Vary the Mode of Action (*Variar de tenor en el obrar*)
xviii. Application and Ability (*Aplicacion y Minerva*)
xix. Arouse no Exaggerated Expectations on entering (*No entrar con sobrada expectation*)
xx. A Man of the Age (*Hombre en su siglo*)
xxi. The Art of being Lucky (*Arte para ser dichoso*)
xxii. A Man of Knowledge to the Point (*Hombre de plausibles noticias*)

xxiii. Be Spotless (*No tener algun desdoro*)

xxiv. Keep the Imagination under Control (*Templar la imaginacion*)

xxv. Know how to take a Hint (*Buen entendedor*)

xxvi. Find out each Man's Thumbscrew (*Hallarle su torcedor á cada uno*)

xxvii. Prize Intensity more than Extent (*Pagarse mas de Intenciones que de Extenciones*)

xxviii Common in Nothing (*En nada vulgar*)

xxix. A Man of Rectitude (*Hombre de entereza*)

xxx. Have naught to do with Occupations of Ill-repute (*No hazer profesion de empleos desautorizados*)

xxxi. Select the Lucky and avoid the Unlucky (*Conocer los afortunados para la election y los desdichados para la fuga*)

xxxii. Have the Reputation of being Gracious (*Estar en opinion de dár gusto*)

xxxiii. Know how to Withdraw (*Saber abstraer*)

xxxiv. Know your strongest Point (*Conocer su realce Rey*)

xxxv. Think over Things, most over the most Important (*Hazer concepto y mas de lo que importa mas*)

xxxvi. In Acting or Refraining, weigh your Luck (*Tener tanteada su Fortuna, para el proceder, para desempeñarse*)

xxxvii. Keep a Store of Sarcasms, and know how to use them (*Conocer y saber usar de las varrillas*)

xxxviii. Leave your Luck while Winning (*Saberse dexar ganando con la fortuna*)

xxxix. Recognize when Things are ripe, and then enjoy them (*Conocer las cosas en su punto, en su sazon y saberlas lograr*)

xl. The Goodwill of People (*Gracia de las gentes*)

xli. Never Exaggerate (*Nunca exagerar*)

xlii. Born to command (*Del natural Imperio*)

xliii. Think with the Few and speak with the Many (*Sentir con los menos y hablar con los mas*)

xliv. Sympathy with great Minds (*Simpatía con los grandes varones*)

xiv. Use, but do not abuse, Cunning (*Usar, no abusar de las reflexas*)

xlvi. Master your Antipathies (*Corregir su antipatia*)

xlvii. Avoid "Affairs of Honor" (*Huir los empeño*)

xlviii. Be Thorough (*Hombre con fondos*)

xlix. Observation and judgment (*Hombre juyzioso y notante*)

l. Never lose Self-respect (*Nunca perderse el respeto á sí mismo*)

li. Know how to Choose well (*Hombre de buena election*)

lii. Never be put out (*Nunca descomponerse*)

liii. Diligent and Intelligent (*Diligente y inteligente*)

liv. Know how to show your Teeth (*Tener brios á lo cuerdo*)

lv. Wait (*Hombre de espera*)

lvi. Have Presence of Mind (*Tener buenos repentes*)

lvii. Slow and Sure (*Mas seguros son los pensados*)
lviii. Adapt Yourself to your Company (*Saberse atemperar*)
lix. Finish off well (*Hombre de buen dexo*)
lx. A Sound judgment (*Buenos dictamenes*)
lxi. To Excel in what is Excellent (*Eminencia en lo mejor*)
lxii. Use good Instruments (*Obrar con buenos instrumentos*)
lxiii. To be the First of the Kind is an Excellence (*Excelencia de primero*)
lxiv. Avoid Worry (*Saberse escusar pesares*)
lxv. Elevated Taste (*Gusto relevante*)
lxvi. See that Things end well (*Atencion que salgan bien las cosas*)
lxvii. Prefer Callings en Evidence (*Preferir los empleos plausibles*)
lxviii. It is better to help with Intelligence than with Memory (*Dar entendimiento es de mas primor que el dár memoria*)
lxix. Do not give way to every common Impulse (*No rendirse á un vulgar humor*)
lxx. Know how to Refuse (*Saber negar*)
lxxi. Do not Vacillate (*No ser desigual*)
lxxii. Be Resolute (*Hombre de resolution*)
lxxiii. Utilise Slips (*Saber usar del desliz*)
lxxiv. Do not be Unsociable (*No ser intratable*)
lxxv. Choose an Heroic Ideal (*Elegir idea heroyca*)
lxxvi. Do not always be jesting (*No estár siempre de burlas*)
lxxvii. Be all Things to all Men (*Saber hazerse á todos*)
lxxviii. The Art of undertaking Things (*Arte en el intentar*)
lxxix. A Genial Disposition (*Genio genial*)
lxxx. Take care to get Information (*Atencion al informarse*)
lxxxi. Renew your Brilliance (*Usar el renovar su lucimiento*)
lxxxii. Drain Nothing to the Dregs, neither Good nor Ill (*Nunca apurar, ni el mal, ni el bien*)
lxxxiii. Allow Yourself some venial Fault (*Permitese algun venial desliz*)
lxxxiv. Make use of your Enemies (*Saber usar de los enemigos*)
lxxxv. Do not play Manille (*No ser malilla*)
lxxxvi. Prevent Scandal (*Prevenir las malas vozes*)
lxxxvii. Culture and Elegance (*Cultura y aliño*)
lxxxviii. Let your Behavior be Fine and Noble (*Sea el trato por mayor procurando la sublimida en él*)
lxxxix. Know Yourself (*Comprehension de sí*)
xc. The Secret of Long Life (*Arte para vivir mucho*)
xci. Never set to work at Anything if you have any Doubts of its Prudence (*Obrar siempre sin escrupolos de imprudencia*)
xcii. Transcendant Wisdom (*Seso transcendental*)
xciii. Versatility (*Hombre universal*)
xciv. Keep the extent of your Abilities unknown (*Incomprehensibilidad*

de caudal)

xcv. Keep Expectation alive (*Saber entretenir la expectation*)

xcvi. The highest Discretion (*De la gran sinderesis*)

xcvii. Obtain and preserve a Reputation (*Conseguir y conservar la reputation*)

xcviii. Write your Intentions in Cypher (*Cifrar la voluntad*)

xcix. Reality and Appearance (*Realidad y aparencia*)

c. A Man without Illusions, a wise Christian, a philosophic Courtier (*Varon desengañado, Christiana sabio, Cortesano filosofo*)

ci. One half of the World laughs at the other, and Fools are they all (*La mitad del mundo se está riendo á la otra mitad, con necedad de todos*)

cii. Be able to stomach big slices of Luck (*Estomago para grander bocados de la fortuna*)

ciii. Let each keep up his Dignity (*Cada uno la magestad en su modo*)

civ. Try your hand at Office (*Tener tomado el pulso á los empleos*)

cv. Don't be a Bore (*No cansar*)

cvi. Do not parade your Position (*No afectar la fortuna*)

cvii. Show no Self-satisfaction (*No mostrar satisfaccion de sí*)

cviii. The Path to Greatness is along with Others (*Atajo para ser persona, saber ladear*)

cix. Be not Censorious (*No ser acriminador*)

cx. Do not wait till you are a Sinking Sun (*No aguardar á ser sol que se pone*)

cxi. Have Friends (*Tener amigos*)

cxii. Gain Good-will (*Ganar la pia aficcion*)

cxiii. In Prosperity prepare for Adversity (*Prevenirse en la fortuna prospera para la adversa*)

cxiv. Never Compete (*Nunca competir*)

cxv. Get used to the Failings of your Familiars (*Hazerse á las malas condiciones de los familiares*)

cxvi. Only act with Honorable Men (*Tratar siempre con gente de obligaciones*)

cxvii. Never talk of Yourself (*Nunca hablar de sí*)

cxviii. Acquire the Reputation of Courtesy (*Cobrar fama de cortés*)

cxix. Avoid becoming Disliked (*No hazerse de mal querer*)

cxx. Live Practically (*Vivir á lo platico*)

cxxi. Do not make a Business of what is no Business (*No hazar negocio del no negocio*)

cxxii. Distinction in Speech and Action (*Señorio en el dezir y en el hazar*)

cxxiii. Avoid Affectation (*Hombre desafectado*)

cxxiv. Get Yourself missed (*Llegar á ser deseados*)

cxxv. Do not be a Black List (*No ser libro verde*)

cxxvi. Folly consists not in committing Folly, but in not hiding it when committed (*No es necio el que haze la necedad, sino el que hecha no la sabe encubrir*)

cxxvii. Grace in Everything (*El despojo en todo*)

cxxviii. Highmindedness (*Alteza de animo*)

cxxix. Never Complain (*Nunca quexarse*)

cxxx. Do and be seen Doing (*Hazer y hazer parecer*)

cxxxi. Nobility of Feeling (*Galantería de condition*)

cxxxii. Revise your Judgments (*Usar del reconsejo*)

cxxxiii. Better Mad with the rest of the World than Wise alone (*Antes loco con todos que cuerdo á solas*)

cxxxiv. Double your Resources (*Doblar los requisitos de la vida*)

cxxxv. Do not nourish the Spirit of Contradiction (*No tenga espiritu de contradicion*)

cxxxvi. Post Yourself in the Centre of Things (*Ponerse bien en las materias*)

cxxxvii. The Sage should be Self-sufficing (*Bastase á sí mismo el sabio*)

cxxxviii. The Art of letting Things alone (*Arte de dexar estár*)

cxxxix. Recognize unlucky Days (*Conocer el dia aziago*)

cxl. Find the Good in a Thing at once (*Hallar luego con lo buena en cada cosa*)

cxli. Do not listen to Yourself (*No escucharse*)

cxlii. Never from Obstinacy take the Wrong Side because your Opponent has anticipated you in taking the Right One (*Nunca por tema seguir el peor partido porque el contrario se adelantó y escogeó el mejor*)

cxliii. Never become Paradoxical in order to avoid the Trite (*No dár en paradoxo por huir de vulgar*)

cxliv. Begin with Another's to end with your Own (*Entrar con la agena para salir con la suya*)

cxlv. Do not show your wounded Finger (*No descubrir el dedo malo*)

cxlvi. Look into the Interior of Things (*Mirar por dentro*)

cxlvii. Do not be Inaccessible (*No ser inaccessible*)

cxlviii. Have the Art of Conversation (*Tener el arte de conversar*)

cxlix. Know how to put off Ills on Others (*Saber declinar á otro los males*)

cl. Know how to get your Price for Things (*Saber vender sus cosas*)

cli. Think beforehand (*Pensar anticipado*)

clii. Never have a Companion who casts you in the Shade (*Nunca acompañarse con quien que pueda deslucir*)

cliii. Beware of entering where there is a great Gap to be filled (*Huya de entrar á llenar grandes vacios*)

cliv. Do not Believe, or Like, lightly (*No ser facil en creer ni en querer*)

clv. The Art of getting into a Passion (*Arte en el apassionarse*) clvi. Select your friends (*Amigos de eleccion*)

clvii. Do not make Mistakes about Character (*No engañarse en las personas*)

clviii. Make use of your Friends (*Saber usar de los amigos*)

clix. Put up with Fools (*Saber sufrir necios*)

clx. Be careful in Speaking (*Hablar de atento*)

clxi. Know your pet Faults (*Conocer los defectos dulces*)

clxii. How to triumph over Rivals and Detractors (*Saber triunfar de la emulation y malevolencia*)

clxiii. Never, from Sympathy with the unfortunate, involve Yourself in his Fate (*Nunca por la compassion del infeliz se ha de incurrir en la desgracia del afortunado*)

clxiv. Throw Straws in the Air (*Echar al ayre algunas cosas*)

clxv. Wage War Honorably (*Hazer buena guerra*)

clxvi. Distinguish the Man of Words from the Man of Deeds (*Diferenciar el hombre de palabras del de obras*)

clxvii. Know how to take your own Part (*Saber se ayudar*)

clxviii. Do not indulge in the Eccentricities of Folly (*No dár en monstruo de la necedad*)

clxix. Be more careful not to Miss once than to Hit a hundred times (*Atencion á no errar una mas que á acertar ciento*)

clxx. In all Things keep Something in Reserve (*Usar del retén en todas las cosas*)

clxxi. Waste not Influence (*No gastar el favor*)

clxxii. Never contend with a Man who has nothing to Lose (*No empeñarse con quien no tiene que perder*)

clxxiii. Do not be Glass in Intercourse, still less in Friendship (*No ser de vitrio en el trato y menos en la amistad*)

clxxiv. Do not live in a Hurry (*No vivir apriesa*)

clxxv. A Solid Man (*Hombre substancial*)

clxxvi. Have Knowledge, or know those that have Knowledge (*Saber o escuchar á quien sabe*)

clxxvii. Avoid Familiarities in Intercourse (*Escusar llanezas en el trato*)

clxxviii. Trust your Heart (*Creer al coraçon*)

clxxix. Reticence is the Seal of Capacity (*La retentiva es el sello de la capacidad*)

clxxx. Never guide the Enemy to what he has to do (*Nunca regirse por lo que el enemigo avia de hazer*)

clxxxi. The Truth, but not the whole Truth (*Sin mentir, no dezir todas las verdades*)

clxxxii. A Grain of Boldness in Everything (*Un grano de audacia con todo*)

clxxxiii. Do not hold your Views too firmly (*No aprender fuertemente*)

clxxxiv. Do not be Ceremonious (*No ser ceremonial*)

clxxxv. Never stake your Credit on a single Cast (*Nunca exponer el credito á la prueba de sola una vez*)

clxxxvi. Recognize Faults, however high placed (*Conocer los defectos por mas autorizados que ester*)

clxxxvii. Do pleasant Things Yourself, unpleasant things through Others (*Todo lo favorable, obrarlo por sí, todo lo odioso, por terceros*)

clxxxviii. Be the Bearer of Praise (*Traer que alabar*)

clxxxix. Utilise Another's Wants (*Valerse de la privacion agena*)

cxc. Find Consolation in all Things (*Hallar el consuelo en todo*)

cxci. Do not take Payment in Politeness (*No pagarse de la mucha cortesia*)

cxcii. Peaceful Life, a long Life (*Hombre de gran paz hombre de mucha vida*)

cxciii. Watch him that begins with Another's to end with his Own (*Atencion al que entra con agena por salir á la suya*)

cxciv. Have reasonable Views of Yourself and of your Affairs (*Concebir de sí y de sus cosas cuerdamente*)

cxcv. Know how to Appreciate (*Saber estimar*)

cxcvi. Know your ruling Star (*Conocer su estrella*)

cxcvii. Do not carry Fools on your Back (*Nunca embaraçarse con los necios*)

cxcvii. Know how to transplant Yourself (*Saberse transplantar*)

cxcix. To find a proper Place by Merit, not by Presumption (*Saberse hazer lugar á lo cuerdo, no á lo entremetido*)

cc. Leave Something to wish for (*Tener que desear*)

cci. They are all Fools who seem so besides half the rest (*Son tontos todos los que lo parecen y la mitad de los que no le parecen*)

ccii. Words and Deeds make the Perfect Man (*Dichos y hechos hazen un varon consumado*)

cciii. Know the great Men of your Age (*Conocer las eminencias de su siglo*)

cciv. Attempt easy Tasks as if they were difficult, and difficult as if they were easy (*Lo facil se ha de emprender como dificultoso y lo dificultoso como facil*)

ccv. Know how to play the Card of Contempt (*Saber jugar del desprechio*)

ccvi. Know that there are vulgar Natures everywhere (*Sepase que ay vulgo en todas partes*)

ccvii. Be Moderate (*Usar del reporte*)

ccviii. Do not die of the Fools' Disease (*No morir de achaque de necio*)

ccix. Keep Yourself free from common Follies (*Librarse de las comunes necedades*)

ccx. Know how to play the Card of Truth (*Saber jugar de la verdad*)

ccxi. In Heaven all is bliss (*En el cielo todo es contento*) ccxii. Keep to Yourself the final Touches of your Art (*Reservarse siempre las ultimas tretas del arte*)

ccxiii. Know how to Contradict (*Saber contradecir*)

ccxiv. Do not turn one Blunder into two (*No hazer de una necedad dos*)

ccxv. Watch him that acts on Second Thoughts (*Atencion al que llega de segunda intencion*)

ccxvi. Be Expressive (*Tener la declarativa*)

ccxvii. Neither Love nor Hate for ever (*No se ha de querer ni aborrecer para siempre*)

ccxviii. Never act from Obstinacy but from Knowledge (*Nunca obrar por tema sino por intencion*)

ccxix. Do not pass for a Hypocrite (*No ser tenido por hombre de artificio*)

ccxx. If you cannot clothe yourself in Lionskin use Foxpelt (*Quando no puede uno vestirse la piel del Leon, vestase la de la Vulpeja*)

ccxxi. Do not seize Occasions to embarrass Yourself or Others (*No ser ocasionado ni para empeñarse, ni para empeñar*)

ccxxii. Reserve is proof of Prudence (*Hombre detenido evidencia de prudente*)

ccxxiii. Be not Eccentric (*No ser muy individuado*)

ccxxiv. Never take Things against the Grain (*Saber tomar las cosas nunca al repelo*)

ccxxv. Know your chief Fault (*Conocer su defecto Rey*)

ccxxvi. Take care to be Obliging (*Atencion á obligar*)

ccxxvii. Do not be the Slave of First Impressions (*No ser de primera Impression*)

ccxxviii. Do not be a Scandalmonger (*No tener voz de mala voz*)

ccxxix. Plan out your Life wisely (*Saber repartir su vida á lo discreto*)

ccxxx. Open your Eyes betimes (*Abrir los ojos con tiempo*)

ccxxxi. Never let Things be seen half-finished (*Nunca permitir á medio hazer las cosas*)

ccxxxii. Have a Touch of the Trader (*Tener un punto de negociante*)

ccxxxiii. Let not the proffered Morsel be distasteful (*No errarle el golpe al gusto*)

ccxxxiv. Never trust your Honor to another, unless you have his in Pledge (*Nunca fiar reputacion sin prendas de honra agena*)

ccxxxv. Know how to Ask (*Saber pedir*)

ccxxxvi. Make an Obligation beforehand of what would have to be a Reward afterwards (*Hazer obligation antes de lo que havia de ser premio despues*)

ccxxxvii. Never share the Secrets of your Superiors (*Nunca partir secretos con mayores*)

ccxxxviii. Know what is wanting in Yourself (*Conocer la pieza que falta*)

ccxxxix. Do not be Captious (*No ser reagudo*)

ccxl. Make use of Folly (*Saber usar de la necedad*)

ccxli. Put up with Raillery, but do not practise it (*Las burlas sufrirlas, pero no usarlas*)

ccxlii. Push Advantages (*Seguir los alcançes*)

ccxliii. Do not be too much of a Dove (*No ser todo colombino*)

ccxliv. Create a feeling of Obligation (*Saber obligar*)

ccxlv. Original and out-of-the-way Views (*Discurrir tal vez á lo singular y fuera de lo comun*)

ccxlvi. Never offer Satisfaction unless it is demanded (*Nunca dár satisfacion á quien no la pedia*)

ccxlvii. Know a little more, Live a little less (*Saber un poco mas, y vivir un poco menos*)

ccxlviii. Do not go with the last Speaker (*No se le lleve el ultimo*)

ccxlix. Never begin Life with what should end it (*No començar á vivir por donde se ha de acabar*)

ccl. When to change the Conversation (*Quando se ha de discurrir a reves*)

ccli. Use human Means as if there were no divine ones, and divine as if there were no human ones (*Hanse de procurar los medios humanos como sino huviesse Divinos, y los Divinos como sino huviesse humanos*)

cclii. Neither belong entirely to Yourself nor entirely to Others (*Ni todo suyo ni todo ageno*)

ccliii. Do not Explain overmuch (*No allanarse sobrado en el concepto*)

ccliv. Never despise an Evil, however small (*No despreciar el mal por poco*)

cclv. Do Good a little at a time, but often (*Saber hazer el bien poco y muchas vezes*)

cclvi. Go armed against Discourtesy (*Ir siempre prevenido contra los discorteses*)

cclvii. Never let Matters come to a Rupture (*Nunca llegar á rompimiento*)

cclviii. Find out some one to share your Troubles (*Buscar quien le ayude a llevar las infelicidades*)

cclix. Anticipate Injuries and turn them into Favors (*Prevenir las injurias y hazer dellas favores*)

cclx. We belong to none and none to us entirely (*Ni será ni tendrá á ninguno todo por suyo*)

cclxi. Do not follow up a Folly (*No proseguir la necedad*)

cclxii. Be able to Forget (*Saber olvidar*)

cclxiii. Many Things of Taste one should not possess oneself (*Muchas cosas de gusto no se han de poseer en propricdad*)

cclxiv. Have no careless Days (*No tenga dias de descuydo*)

cclxv. Set those under you difficult Tasks (*Saber empeñar los dependientes*) cclxvi. Do not become Bad from sheer Goodness (*No ser malo de puro bueno*)

cclxvii. Silken Words, Sugared Manners (*Palabras de seda con suavidad de condition*)

cclxviii. The Wise does at once what the Fool does at last (*Haga al principio el cuerdo lo que el necio al fin*)

cclxix. Make use of the Novelty of your Position (*Valgase de su novedad*)

cclxx. Do not condemn alone that which pleases all (*No condenar solo lo que á muchos agrada*)

cclxxi. In every Occupation if you know little stick to the safest (*El que supiere poco tengase siempre á lo mas seguro en toda profession*)

cclxxii. Sell The Things the Tariff of Courtesy (*Vender las cosas á precio de cortesia*)

cclxxiii. Comprehend their Dispositions with whom you deal (*Comprehension de los genios con quien trata*)

cclxxiv. Be Attractive (*Tener la atractiva*)

cclxxv. Join in the Game as far as Decency permits (*Corriente pero no indecente*)

cclxxvi. Know how to renew your Character (*Saber renovar el genio*)

cclxxvii. Display Yourself (*Hombre de ostentacion*)

cclxxviii. Avoid Notoriety in all Things (*Huir la nota en toda*)

cclxxix. Do not contradict the Contradicter (*No dezir al contradezir*)

cclxxx. Be Trustworthy (*Hombre de ley*)

cclxxxi. Find Favor with Men of Sense (*Gracia con los entendidos*)

cclxxxii. Make use of Absence to make more esteemed or yourself valued (*Usar de la ausencia á para el respecta, ó para la estimation*)

cclxxxiii. Have the Gift of Discovery (*Hombre de Inventiva*)

cclxxxiv. Do not be Importunate (*No ser entremedido*)

cclxxxv. Never die of another's Ill-luck (*No perecer de desdicha agena*)

cclxxxvi. Do not become responsible for all or for every one (*No dexarse obligar del todo ni de todos*)

cclxxxvii. Never act in a Passion (*Nunca obrar apassionado*)

cclxxxviii. Live for the Moment (*Vivir á la ocasion*)

cclxxxix. Nothing depreciates a Man more than to show he is a Man like other Men (*El mayor desdoro de un hombre es dár muestras de que es hombre*)

ccxc. 'Tis a piece of Good Fortune to combine Men's Love and Respect (*Es felicidad juntar el aprecio con el afecta*)

ccxci. Know how to Test (*Saber hazer la tentativa*)

ccxcii. Let your personal Qualities surpass those of your Office (*Vença el natural las obligaciones del empleo*)

ccxciii. Maturity (*De la madurez*)

ccxciv. Be moderate in your Views (*Moderarse en el sentir*)

ccxcv. Do not Affect what you have not effected (*No hazañero sino hazañoso*)

ccxcvi. Noble Qualities (*Varon de prendas y magestuosas*)

ccxcvii. Act always as if your Acts were seen (*Obrar siempre como á vista*)

ccxcviii. Three Things go to a Prodigy (*Tres cosas hazer un prodigio*)

ccxcix. Leave off Hungry (*Dexar con hambre*)

ccc. In one word, be a Saint (*En una palabra santo*)

To the Reader

No laws for the just, no counsels for the wise. Yet no one ever knew as much as he had need. One thing you must forgive, another, thank me for. I have called this manual of worldly wisdom an Oracle, for it is one in curtness and sententiousness. On the other hand, I offer you in one all the twelve works of Gracian. Each of these is so highly thought of that his Prudent Man had scarcely appeared in Spain than it was enjoyed among the French, in whose language it was translated and at whose court it was printed. May this be Wisdom's bill of fare at the banquet of her sages, in which she inscribes the items of the feast of reason to be found in Gracian's other works.

DON VINCENCIO JUAN DE LASTANOSA.

The Art of Worldly Wisdom

i. *Everything is at its Acme*;

especially the art of making one's way in the world. There is more required nowadays to make a single wise man than formerly to make Seven Sages, and more is needed nowadays to deal with a single person than was required with a whole people in former times.

ii. *Character and Intellect*:

the two poles of our capacity; one without the other is but halfway to happiness. Intellect sufficeth not, character is also needed. On the other hand, it is the fool's misfortune, to fail in obtaining the position, the employment, the neighborhood, and the circle of friends that suit him.

iii. *Keep Matters for a Time in Suspense.*

Admiration at their novelty heightens the value of your achievements, It is both useless and insipid to play with the cards on the table. If you do not declare yourself immediately, you arouse expectation, especially when the importance of your position makes you the object of general attention. Mix a little mystery with everything, and the very mystery arouses veneration. And when you explain, be not too explicit, just as you do not expose your inmost thoughts in ordinary intercourse. Cautious silence is the holy of holies of worldly wisdom. A resolution declared is never highly thought of; it only leaves room for criticism. And if it happens to fail, you are doubly unfortunate. Besides you imitate the Divine way when you cause men to wonder and watch.

iv. *Knowledge and Courage*

are the elements of Greatness. They give immortality, because they are immortal. Each is as much as he knows, and the wise can do anything. A man without knowledge, a world without light. Wisdom and strength, eyes and hands. Knowledge without courage is sterile.

v. *Create a Feeling of Dependence.*

Not he that adorns but he that adores makes a divinity. The wise man would rather see men needing him than thanking him. To keep them on the threshold of hope is diplomatic, to trust to their gratitude boorish; hope has a good memory, gratitude a bad one. More is to be got from dependence than from courtesy. He that has satisfied his thirst turns his back on the well, and the orange once sucked falls from the golden platter into the waste-basket. When dependence disappears, good behavior goes with it as well as respect. Let it be one of the chief lessons of experience to keep hope alive without entirely satisfying it, by preserving it to make oneself always needed even by a patron on the throne. But let not silence be carried to excess lest you go wrong, nor let another's failing grow incurable for the sake of your own advantage.

vi. *A Man at his Highest Point.*

We are not born perfect: every day we develop in our personality and in our calling till we reach the highest point of our completed being, to the full round of our accomplishments, of our excellences. This is known by the purity of our taste, the clearness of our thought, the maturity of our judgment, and the firmness of our will. Some never arrive at being complete; somewhat is always awanting: others ripen late. The complete man, wise in speech, prudent in act, is admitted to the familiar intimacy of discreet persons, is even sought for by them.

vii. *Avoid Victories over Superiors.*

All victories breed hate, and that over your superior is foolish or fatal. Superiority is always detested, *à fortiori* superiority over superiority. Caution can gloss over common advantages; for example, good looks may be cloaked by careless attire. There be some that will grant you precedence in good luck or good temper, but none in good sense, least of all a prince; for good sense is a royal prerogative, any claim to that is a case of *lèse majesté*. They are princes, and wish to be so in that most princely of qualities. They will allow a man to help them but not to surpass them, and will have any advice tendered them appear like a recollection of something they have forgotten rather than as a guide to something they cannot find. The stars teach us this finesse with happy tact; though they are his children and brilliant like him, they never rival the brilliancy of the sun.

viii. *To be without Passions.*

'Tis a privilege of the highest order of mind. Their very eminence redeems them from being affected by transient and low impulses. There is no higher rule than that over oneself, over one's impulses: there is the triumph of free will. While passion rules the character, no aiming at high office; the less the higher. It is the only refined way of avoiding scandals; nay, 'tis the shortest way back to good repute.

ix. *Avoid the Faults of your Nation.*

Water shares the good or bad qualities of the strata through which it flows, and man those of the climate in which he is born. Some owe more than others to their native land, because there is a more favorable sky in the zenith. There is not a nation even among the most civilised that has not some fault peculiar to itself which other nations blame by way of boast or as a warning. 'Tis a triumph of cleverness to correct in oneself such national failings, or even to hide them: you get great credit for being unique among your fellows, and as it is less expected of you it is esteemed the more. There are also family failings as well as faults of position, of office or of age. If these all meet in one person and are not carefully guarded against, they make an intolerable monster.

x. *Fortune and Fame.*

Where the one is fickle the other is enduring. The first for life, the second afterwards; the one against envy, the other against oblivion. Fortune is desired, at times assisted: fame is earned. The desire for fame springs from man's best part. It was and is the sister of the giants; it always goes to extremes—horrible monsters or brilliant prodigies.

xi. *Cultivate those who can teach you.*

Let friendly intercourse be a school of knowledge, and culture be taught through conversation: thus you make your friends your teachers and mingle the pleasures of conversation with the advantages of instruction. Sensible persons thus enjoy alternating pleasures: they reap applause for what they say, and gain instruction from what they hear. We are always attracted to others by our own interest, but in this case it is of a higher kind. Wise men frequent the houses of great noblemen not because they are temples of vanity, but as theatres of good breeding. There be gentlemen who have the credit of worldly wisdom, because they are not only themselves oracles of all nobleness by their example and their behavior, but those who surround them form a well-bred academy of worldly wisdom of the best and noblest kind.

xii. *Nature and Art:*

material and workmanship. There is no beauty unadorned and no excellence that would not become barbaric if it were not supported by artifice: this remedies the evil and improves the good. Nature scarcely ever gives us the very best; for that we must have recourse to art. Without this the best of natural dispositions is uncultured, and half is lacking to any excellence if training is absent. Everyone has something unpolished without artificial training, and every kind of excellence needs some polish.

xiii. *Act sometimes on Second Thoughts, sometimes on First Impulse.*

Man's life is a warfare against the malice of men. Sagacity fights with strategic changes of intention: it never does what it threatens, it aims only at escaping notice. It aims in the air with dexterity and strikes home in an unexpected direction, always seeking to conceal its game. It lets a purpose appear in order to attract the opponent's attention, but then turns round and conquers by the unexpected. But a penetrating intelligence anticipates this by watchfulness and lurks in ambush. It always understands the opposite of what the opponent wishes it to understand, and recognizes every feint of guile. It lets the first impulse pass by and waits for the second, or even the third. Sagacity now rises to higher flights on seeing its artifice foreseen, and tries to deceive by truth itself, changes its game in order to change its deceit, and cheats by not cheating, and founds deception on the greatest candor. But the opposing intelligence is on guard with increased watchfulness, and discovers the darkness concealed by the light and deciphers every move, the more subtle because more simple. In this way the guile of the Python combats the far darting rays of Apollo.

xiv. *The Thing Itself and the Way it is done.*

"Substance" is not enough: "accident" is also required, as the scholastics say. A bad manner spoils everything, even reason and justice; a good one supplies everything, gilds a No, sweetens truth, and adds a touch of beauty to old age itself. The *how* plays a large part in affairs, a good manner steals into the affections. Fine behavior is a joy in life, and a pleasant expression helps out of a difficulty in a remarkable way.

xv. *Keep Ministering Spirits.*

It is a privilege of the mighty to surround themselves with the champions of intellect; these extricate them from every fear of ignorance, these worry out for them the moot points of every difficulty. 'Tis a rare greatness to make use of the wise, and far exceeds the barbarous taste of Tigranes, who had a fancy for captive monarchs as his servants. It is a novel kind of supremacy, the best that life can offer, to have as servants by skill those who by nature are our masters. 'Tis a great thing to know, little to live: no real life without knowledge. There is remarkable cleverness in studying without study, in getting much by means of many, and through them all to become wise. Afterwards you speak in the council chamber on behalf of many, and as many sages speak through your mouth as were consulted beforehand: you thus obtain the fame of an oracle by others' toil. Such ministering spirits distil the best books and serve up the quintessence of wisdom. But he that cannot have sages in service should have them for his friends.

xvi. *Knowledge and Good Intentions*

together ensure continuance of success. A fine intellect wedded to a wicked will was always an unnatural monster. A wicked will envenoms all excellences: helped by knowledge it only ruins with greater subtlety. 'Tis a miserable superiority that only results in ruin. Knowledge without sense is double folly.

xvii. *Vary the Mode of Action*;

not always the same way, so as to distract attention, especially if there be a rival. Not always from first impulse; they will soon recognize the uniformity, and by anticipating, frustrate your designs. It is easy to kill a bird on the wing that flies straight: not so one that twists. Nor always act on second thoughts: they can discern the plan the second time. The enemy is on the watch, great skill is required to circumvent him. The gamester never plays the card the opponent expects, still less that which he wants.

xviii. *Application and Ability.*

There is no attaining eminence without both, and where they unite there is the greatest eminence. Mediocrity obtains more with application than superiority without it. Work is the price which is paid for reputation. What costs little is little worth. Even for the highest posts it is only in some cases application that is wanting, rarely the talent. To prefer moderate success in great things than eminence in a humble post has the excuse of a generous mind, but not so to be content with humble mediocrity when you could shine among the highest. Thus nature and art are both needed, and application sets on them the seal.

xix. *Arouse no Exaggerated Expectations on entering.*

It is the usual ill-luck of all celebrities not to fulfill afterwards the expectations beforehand formed of them. The real can never equal the imagined, for it is easy to form ideals but very difficult to realize them. Imagination weds Hope and gives birth to much more than things are in themselves. However great the excellences, they never suffice to fulfill expectations, and as men find themselves disappointed with their exorbitant expectations they are more ready to be disillusionised than to admire. Hope is a great falsifier of truth; let skill guard against this by ensuring that fruition exceeds desire. A few creditable attempts at the beginning are sufficient to arouse curiosity without pledging one to the final object. It is better that reality should surpass the design and is better than was thought. This rule does not apply to the wicked, for the same exaggeration is a great aid to them; they are defeated amid general applause, and what seemed at first extreme ruin comes to be thought quite bearable.

xx. *A Man of the Age.*

The rarest individuals depend on their age. It is not every one that finds the age he deserves, and even when he finds it he does not always know how to utilize it. Some men have been worthy of a better century, for every species of good does not always triumph. Things have their period; even excellences are subject to fashion. The sage has one advantage: he is immortal. If *this* is not his century many others will be.

xxi. *The Art of being Lucky.*

There are rules of luck: it is not all chance with the wise: it can be assisted by care. Some content themselves with placing them-selves confidently at the gate of Fortune, waiting till she opens it. Others do better, and press forward and profit by their clever boldness, reaching the goddess and winning her favor on the wings of their virtue and valor. But on a true philosophy there is no other umpire than virtue and insight; for there is no luck or ill-luck except wisdom and the reverse.

xxii. *A Man of Knowledge to the Point.*

Wise men arm themselves with tasteful and elegant erudition; a practical knowledge of what is going on not of a common kind but more like an expert. They possess a copious store of wise and witty sayings, and of noble deeds, and know how to employ them on fitting occasions. More is often taught by a jest than by the most serious teaching. Pat knowledge helps some more than the seven arts, be they ever so liberal.

xxiii. *Be Spotless*:

the indispensable condition of perfection. Few live without some weak point, either physical or moral, which they pamper because they could easily cure it. The keenness of others often regrets to see a slight defect attaching itself to a whole assembly of elevated qualities, and yet a single cloud can hide the whole of the sun. There are likewise patches on our reputation which ill-will soon finds out and is continually noticing. The highest skill is to transform them into ornament. So Cæsar hid his natural defects with the laurel.

xxiv. *Keep the Imagination under Control*;

sometimes correcting, sometimes assisting it. For it is all-important for our happiness, and even sets the reason right. It can tyrannize, and is not content with looking on, but influences and even often dominates life, causing it to be happy or burdensome according to the folly to which it leads. For it makes us either contented or discontented with ourselves. Before some it continually holds up the penalties of action, and becomes the mortifying lash of these fools. To others it promises happiness and adventure with blissful delusion. It can do all this unless the most prudent self-control keeps it in subjection.

xxv. *Know how to take a Hint.*

'Twas once the art of arts to be able to discourse; now 'tis no longer sufficient. We must know how to take a hint, especially in disabusing ourselves. He cannot make himself understood who does not himself easily understand. But on the other hand there are pretended diviners of the heart and lynxes of the intentions. The very truths which concern us most can only be half spoken, but with attention we can grasp the whole meaning. When you hear anything favorable keep a tight rein on your credulity; if unfavorable, give it the spur.

xxvi. *Find out each Man's Thumbscrew.*

'Tis the art of setting their wills in action. It needs more skill than resolution. You must know where to get at any one. Every volition has a special motive which varies according to taste. All men are idolaters, some of fame, others of self-interest, most of pleasure. Skill consists in knowing these idols in order to bring them into play. Knowing any man's mainspring of motive you have as it were the key to his will. Have resort to primary motors, which are not always the highest but more often the lowest part of his nature: there are more dispositions badly organized than well. First guess a man's ruling passion, appeal to it by a word, set it in motion by temptation, and you will infallibly give checkmate to his freedom of will.

xxvii. *Prize Intensity more than Extent.*

Excellence resides in quality not in quantity. The best is always few and rare: much lowers value. Even among men giants are commonly the real dwarfs. Some reckon books by the thickness, as if they were written to try the brawn more than the brain. Extent alone never rises above mediocrity: it is the misfortune of universal geniuses that in attempting to be at home everywhere, are so nowhere. Intensity gives eminence, and rises to the heroic in matters sublime.

xxviii. *Common in Nothing.*

First, not in taste. O great and wise, to be ill at ease when your deeds please the mob! The excesses of popular applause never satisfy the sensible. Some there are such chameleons of popularity that they find enjoyment not in the sweet savors of Apollo but in the breath of the mob. Secondly, not in intelligence. Take no pleasure in the wonder of the mob, for ignorance never gets beyond wonder. While vulgar folly wonders wisdom watches for the trick.

xxix. *A Man of Rectitude*

clings to the sect of right with such tenacity of purpose that neither the passions of the mob nor the violence of the tyrant can ever cause him to transgress the bounds of right. But who shall be such a Phœnix of equity? What a scanty following has rectitude! Many praise it indeed, but—for others. Others follow it till danger threatens; then the false deny it, the politic conceal it. For it cares not if it fights with friendship, power, or even self-interest: then comes the danger of desertion. Then astute men make plausible distinctions so as not to stand in the way of their superiors or of reasons of state. But the straightforward and constant regard dissimulation as a kind of treason, and set more store on tenacity than on sagacity. Such are always to be found on the side of truth, and if they desert a party, they do not change from fickleness, but because the others have first deserted truth.

xxx. *Have naught to do with Occupations of Ill-repute,*

still less with fads that bring more notoriety than repute. There are many fanciful sects, and from all the prudent man has to flee. There are bizarre tastes that always take to their heart all that wise men repudiate; they live in love with singularity. This may make them well known indeed, but more as objects of ridicule than of repute. A cautious man does not even make profession of his wisdom, still less of those matters that make their followers ridiculous. These need not be specified, for common contempt has sufficiently singled them out.

xxxi. *Select the Lucky and avoid the Unlucky.*

Ill-luck is generally the penalty of folly, and there is no disease so contagious to those who share in it. Never open the door to a lesser evil, for other and greater ones invariably slink in after it. The greatest skill at cards is to know when to discard; the smallest of current trumps is worth more than the ace of trumps of the last game. When in doubt, follow the suit of the wise and prudent; sooner or later they will win the odd trick.

xxxii. *Have the Reputation of being Gracious.*

'Tis the chief glory of the high and mighty to be gracious, a prerogative of kings to conquer universal goodwill. That is the great advantage of a commanding position—to be able to do more good than others. Those make friends who do friendly acts. On the other hand, there are some who lay themselves out for not being gracious, not on account of the difficulty, but from a bad disposition. In all things they are the opposite of Divine grace.

xxxiii. *Know how to Withdraw.*

If it is a great lesson in life to know how to deny, it is a still greater to know how to deny oneself as regards both affairs and persons. There are extraneous occupations which eat away precious time. To be occupied in what does not concern you is worse than doing nothing. It is not enough for a careful man not to interfere with others, he must see that they do not interfere with him. One is not obliged to belong so much to all as not to belong at all to oneself. So with friends, their help should not be abused or more demanded from them than they themselves will grant. All excess is a failing, but above all in personal intercourse. A wise moderation in this best preserves the goodwill and esteem of all, for by this means that precious boon of courtesy is not gradually worn away. Thus you preserve your genius free to select the elect, and never sin against the unwritten laws of good taste.

xxxiv. *Know your strongest Point—*

your pre-eminent gift; cultivate that and you will assist the rest. Everyone would have excelled in something if he had known his strong point. Notice in what quality you surpass, and take charge of that. In some judgment excels, in others valor. Most do violence to their natural aptitude, and thus attain superiority in nothing. Time disillusionises us too late of what first flattered the passions.

xxv. *Think over Things, most over the most Important.*

All fools come to grief from want of thought. They never see even the half of things, and as they do not observe their own loss or gain, still less do they apply any diligence to them. Some make much of what imports little and little of much, always weighing in the wrong scale. Many never lose their common sense, because they have none to lose. There are matters which should be observed with the closest attention of the mind, and thenceforth kept in its lowest depths. The wise man thinks over everything, but with a difference, most profoundly where there is some profound difficulty, and thinks that perhaps there is more in it than he thinks. Thus his comprehension extends as far as his apprehension.

xxxvi. *In Acting or Refraining, weigh your Luck.*

More depends on that than on noticing your temperament. If he is a fool who at forty applies to Hippocrates for health, still more is he one who then first applies to Seneca for wisdom. It is a great piece of skill to know how to guide your luck even while waiting for it. For something is to be done with it by waiting so as to use it at the proper moment, since it has periods and offers opportunities, though one cannot calculate its path, its steps are so irregular. When you find Fortune favorable, stride boldly forward, for she favors the bold and, being a woman, the young. But if you have bad luck, keep retired so as not to redouble the influence of your unlucky star.

xxxvii. *Keep a Store of Sarcasms, and know how to use them.*

This is the point of greatest tact in human intercourse. Such sarcasms are often thrown out to test men's moods, and by their means one often obtains the most subtle and penetrating touchstone of the heart. Other sarcasms are malicious, insolent, poisoned by envy or envenomed by passion, unexpected flashes which destroy at once all favor and esteem. Struck by the slightest word of this kind, many fall away from the closest intimacy with superiors or inferiors which could not be the slightest shaken by a whole conspiracy of popular insinuation or private malevolence. Other sarcasms, on the other hand, work favorably, confirming and assisting one's reputation. But the greater the skill with which they are launched, the greater the caution with which they should be received and the foresight with which they should he foreseen. For here a knowledge of the evil is in itself a means of defense, and a shot foreseen always misses its mark.

xxxviii. *Leave your Luck while Winning.*

All the best players do it. A fine retreat is as good as a gallant attack. Bring your exploits under cover when there are enough, or even when there are many of them. Luck long lasting was ever suspicious; interrupted seems safer, and is even sweeter to the taste for a little infusion of bitter-sweet. The higher the heap of luck, the greater the risk of a slip, and down comes all. Fortune pays you sometimes for the intensity of her favors by the shortness of their duration. She soon tires of carrying any one long on her shoulders.

xxxix. *Recognize when Things are ripe, and then enjoy them.*

The works of nature all reach a certain point of maturity; up to that they improve, after that they degenerate. Few works of art reach such a point that they cannot be improved. It is an especial privilege of good taste to enjoy everything at its ripest. Not all can do this, nor do all who can know this. There is a ripening point too for fruits of intellect; it is well to know this both for their value in use and for their value in exchange.

xl. *The Goodwill of People.*

'Tis much to gain universal admiration; more, universal love. Something depends on natural disposition, more on practice: the first founds, the second then builds on that foundation. Brilliant parts suffice not, though they are presupposed; win good opinion and 'tis easy to win goodwill. Kindly acts besides are required to produce kindly feelings, doing good with both hands, good words and better deeds, loving so as to be loved. Courtesy is the politic witchery of great personages. First lay hand on deeds and then on pens; words follow swords; for there is goodwill to be won among writers, and it is eternal.

xli. *Never Exaggerate.*

It is an important object of attention not to talk in superlatives, so as neither to offend against truth nor to give a mean idea of one's understanding. Exaggeration is a prodigality of the judgment which shows the narrowness of one's knowledge or one's taste. Praise arouses lively curiosity, begets desire, and if afterwards the value does not correspond to the price, as generally happens, expectation revolts against the deception, and revenges itself by under-estimating the thing recommended and the person recommending. A prudent man goes more cautiously to work, and prefers to err by omission than by commission. Extraordinary things are rare, therefore moderate ordinary valuation. Exaggeration is a branch of lying, and you lose by it the credit of good taste, which is much, and of good sense, which is more.

xlii. *Born to Command.*

It is a secret force of superiority not to have to get on by artful trickery but by an inborn power of rule. All submit to it without knowing why, recognising the secret vigor of connatural authority. Such magisterial spirits are kings by merit and lions by innate privilege. By the esteem which they inspire, they hold the hearts and minds of the rest. If their other qualities permit, such men are born to be the prime motors of the state. They per-form more by a gesture than others by a long harangue.

xliii. *Think with the Few and speak with the Many.*

By swimming against the stream it is impossible to remove error, easy to fall into danger; only a Socrates can undertake it. To dissent from others' views is regarded as an insult, because it is their condemnation. Disgust is doubled on account of the thing blamed and of the person who praised it. Truth is for the few, error is both common and vulgar. The wise man is not known by what he says on the house-tops, for there he speaks not with his own voice but with that of common folly, however much his inmost thoughts may gainsay it. The prudent avoid being contradicted as much as contradicting: though they have their censure ready they are not ready to publish it. Thought is free, force cannot and should not be used to it. The wise man therefore retires into silence, and if he allows himself to come out of it, he does so in the shade and before few and fit persons.

xliv. *Sympathy with great Minds.*

It is an heroic quality to agree with heroes. 'Tis like a miracle of nature for mystery and for use. There is a natural kinship of hearts and minds: its effects are such that vulgar ignorance scents witchcraft. Esteem established, goodwill follows, which at times reaches affection. It persuades without words and obtains without earning. This sympathy is sometimes active, sometimes passive, both alike felicific; the more so, the more sublime. 'Tis a great art to recognize, to distinguish and to utilize this gift. No amount of energy suffices without that favor of nature.

xlv. *Use, but do not abuse, Cunning.*

One ought not to delight in it, still less to boast of it. Everything artificial should be concealed, most of all cunning, which is hated. Deceit is much in use; therefore our caution has to be redoubled, but not so as to show itself, for it arouses distrust, causes much annoy, awakens revenge, and gives rise to more ills than you would imagine. To go to work with caution is of great advantage in action, and there is no greater proof of wisdom. The greatest skill in any deed consists in the sure mastery with which it is executed.

xlvi. *Master your Antipathies.*

We often allow ourselves to take dislikes, and that before we know anything of a person. At times this innate yet vulgar aversion attaches Itself to eminent personalities. Good sense masters this feeling, for there is nothing more discreditable than to dislike those better than ourselves. As sympathy with great men en-nobles us, so dislike to them degrades us.

xlvii. *Avoid "Affairs of Honor"*

—one of the chiefest aims of prudence. In men of great ability the extremes are kept far asunder, so that there is a long distance between them, and they always keep in the middle of their caution, so that they take time to break through it. It is easier to avoid such affairs than to come well out of them. They test our judgment; it is better to avoid them than to conquer in them. One affair of honor leads to another, and may lead to an affair of dishonor. There are men so constituted by nature or by nation that they easily enter upon such obligations. But for him that walks by the light of reason, such a matter requires long thinking over. There is more valor needed not to take up the affair than to conquer in it. When there is one fool ready for the occasion, one may excuse oneself from being the second.

xlviii. *Be Thorough.*

How much depends on the person. The interior must be at least as much as the exterior. There are natures all frontage, like houses that for want of means have the portico of a palace leading to the rooms of a cottage. It is no use boring into such persons, although they bore you, for conversation flags after the first salutation. They prance through the first compliments like Sicilian barbs, but silence soon succeeds, for the flow of words soon ceases where there is no spring of thoughts. Others may be taken in by them because they themselves have but a view of the surface, but not the prudent, who look within them and find nothing there except material for scorn.

xlix. *Observation and Judgment.*

A man with these rules things, not they him. He sounds at once the profoundest depths; he is a phrenologist by means of physiognomy. On seeing a person he understands him and judges of his inmost nature. From a few observations he deciphers the most hidden recesses of his nature. Keen observation, subtle insight, judicious inference: with these he discovers, notices, grasps, and comprehends everything.

l. *Never lose Self-respect,*

or be too familiar with oneself. Let your own right feeling be the true standard of your rectitude, and owe more to the strictness of your own self-judgment than to all external sanctions. Leave off anything unseemly more from regard for your own self-respect than from fear of external authority. Pay regard to that and there is no need of Seneca's imaginary tutor.

li. *Know how to Choose well.*

Most of life depends thereon. It needs good taste and correct judgment, for which neither intellect nor study suffices. To be choice, you must choose, and for this two things are needed: to be able to choose at all, and then to choose the best. There are many men of fecund and subtle mind, of keen judgment, of much learning, and of great observation who yet are at a loss when they come to choose. They always take the worst as if they had tried to go wrong. Thus this is one of the greatest gifts from above.

lii. *Never be put out.*

'Tis a great aim of prudence never to be embarrassed. It is the sign of a real man. Of a noble heart, for magnanimity is not easily put out. The passions are the humors of the soul, and every excess in them weakens prudence; if they overflow through the mouth, the reputation will be in danger. Let a man therefore be so much and so great a master over himself that neither in the most fortunate nor in the most adverse circumstances can anything cause his reputation injury by disturbing his self-possession, but rather enhance it by showing his superiority.

liii. *Diligent and Intelligent.*

Diligence promptly executes what intelligence slowly excogitates. Hurry is the failing of fools; they know not the crucial point and set to work without preparation. On the other hand, the wise more often fail from procrastination; foresight begets deliberation, and remiss action often nullifies prompt judgment. Celerity is the mother of good fortune. He has done much who leaves nothing over till to-morrow. *Festina lente* is a royal motto.

liv. *Know how to show your Teeth.*

Even hares can pull the mane of a dead lion. There is no joke about courage. Give way to the first and you must yield to the second, and so on till the last, and to gain your point at last costs as much trouble as would have gained much more at first. Moral courage exceeds physical; it should be like a sword kept ready for use in the scabbard of caution. It Is the shield of great place; moral cowardice lowers one more than physical. Many have had eminent qualities, yet, for want of a stout heart, they passed inanimate lives and found a tomb in their own sloth. Wise Nature has thoughtfully combined in the bee the sweetness of its honey with the sharpness of its sting.

lv. *Wait.*

It's a sign of a noble heart dowered with patience, never to be in a hurry, never to be in a passion. First be master over yourself if you would be master over others. You must pass through the circumference of time before arriving at the centre of opportunity. A wise reserve seasons the aims and matures the means. Time's crutch effects more than the iron club of Hercules. God Himself chasteneth not with a rod but with time. He[18] spake a great word who said, "Time and I against any two." Fortune herself rewards waiting with the first prize.

lvi. *Have Presence of Mind.*

The child of a happy promptitude of spirit. Owing to this vivacity and wideawakeness there is no fear of danger or mischance. Many reflect much only to go wrong in the end: others attain their aim without thinking of it beforehand. There are natures of Antiperistasis who work best in an emergency. They are like monsters who succeed in all they do offhand, but fail in aught they think over. A thing occurs to

---

[18] Charles V.

them at once or never: for them there is no court of appeal. Celerity wins applause because it proves remarkable capacity; subtlety of judgment, prudence in action.

lvii. *Slow and Sure.*

Early enough if well. Quickly done can be quickly undone. To last an eternity requires an eternity of preparation. Only excellence counts; only achievement endures. Profound intelligence is the only foundation for immortality. Worth much costs much. The precious metals are the heaviest.

lviii. *Adapt Yourself to your Company.*

There is no need to show your ability before every one. Employ no more force than is necessary. Let there be no unnecessary expenditure either of knowledge or of power. The skilful falconer only flies enough birds to serve for the chase. If there is too much display to-day there will be nothing to show to-morrow. Always have some novelty wherewith to dazzle. To show something fresh each day keeps expectation alive and conceals the limits of capacity.

lix. *Finish off well.*

In the house of Fortune, if you enter by the gate of pleasure you must leave by that of sorrow and *vice versâ*. You ought therefore to think of the finish, and attach more importance to a graceful exit than to applause on entrance. 'Tis the common lot of the unlucky to have a very fortunate outset and a very tragic end. The important point is not the vulgar applause on entrance—that comes to nearly all—but the general feeling at exit. Few in life are felt to deserve an encore. Fortune rarely accompanies any one to the door: warmly as she may welcome the coming, she speeds but coldly the parting guest.

lx. *A Sound Judgment.*

Some are born wise, and with this natural advantage enter upon their studies, with a moiety already mastered. With age and experience their reason ripens, and thus they attain a sound judgment. They abhor everything whimsical as leading prudence astray, especially in matters of state, where certainty is so necessary, owing to the importance of the affairs involved., Such men deserve to stand by the helm of state either as pilots or as men at the wheel.

lxi. *To Excel in what is Excellent.*

A great rarity among excellences. You cannot have a great man without something pre-eminent. Mediocrities never win applause. Eminence in some distinguished post distinguishes one from the vulgar mob and ranks us with the elect. To be distinguished in a Small post is to be great in little: the more comfort, the less glory. The highest eminence in great affairs has the royal characteristic of exciting admiration and winning goodwill.

lxii. *Use good Instruments.*

Some would have the subtlety of their wits proven by the meanness of their instruments. 'Tis a dangerous satisfaction, and deserves a fatal punishment. The excellence of a minister never diminished the greatness of his lord. All the glory of exploits reverts to the principal actor; also all the blame. Fame only does business with principals. She does not say, "This had good, that had bad servants," but, "This was a good artist, that a bad one." Let your assistants be selected and tested therefore, for you have to trust to them for an immortality of fame.

lxiii. *To he the First of the Kind is an Excellence,*

and to be eminent in it as well, a double one. To have the first move is a great ad-vantage when the players are equal. Many a man would have been a veritable Phœnix if he had been the first of the sort. Those who come first are the heirs of Fame; the others get only a younger brother's allowance: whatever they do, they cannot persuade the world they are anything more than parrots. The skill of prodigies may find a new path to eminence, but prudence accompanies them all the way. By the novelty of their enterprises sages write their names in the golden book of heroes. Some prefer to be first in things of minor import than second in greater exploits.

lxiv. *Avoid Worry.*

Such prudence brings its own reward. It escapes much, and is thus the midwife of comfort and so of happiness. Neither give nor take bad news unless it can help. Some men's ears are stuffed with the sweets of flattery; others with the bitters of scandal, while some cannot live without a daily annoyance no more than Mithridates could without poison. It is no rule of life to prepare for yourself lifelong trouble in order to give a temporary enjoyment to another, however near and dear.

You never ought to spoil your own chances to please another who advises and keeps out of the affair, and in all cases where to oblige another involves disobliging yourself, 'tis a standing rule that it is better he should suffer now than you afterwards and in vain.

lxv. *Elevated Taste.*

You can train it like the intellect. Full knowledge whets desire and increases enjoyment. You may know a noble spirit by the elevation of his taste: it must be a great thing that can satisfy a great mind. Big bites for big mouths, lofty things for lofty spirits. Before their judgment the bravest tremble, the most perfect lose confidence. Things of the first importance are few; let appreciation be rare. Taste can be imparted by intercourse: great good luck to associate with the highest taste. But do not affect to be dissatisfied with everything: 'tis the extreme of folly, and more odious if from affectation than if from Quixotry. Some would have God create another world and other ideals to satisfy their fantastic imagination.

lxvi. *See that Things end well.*

Some regard more the rigour of the game than the winning of it, but to the world the discredit of the final failure does away with any recognition of the previous care. The victor need not explain. The world does not notice the details of the measures employed; but only the good or ill result. You lose nothing if you gain your end. A good end gilds everything, however unsatisfactory the means. Thus at times it is part of the art of life to transgress the rules of the art, if you cannot end well otherwise.

lxvii. *Prefer Callings "en Evidence."*

Most things depend on the satisfaction of others. Esteem is to excellence what the zephyr is to flowers, the breath of life. There are some callings which gain universal esteem, while others more important are without credit. The former, pursued before the eyes of all, obtain the universal favor; the others, though they are rarer and more valuable, remain obscure and unperceived, honored but not applauded. Among princes conquerors are the most celebrated, and therefore the kings of Aragon earned such applause as warriors, conquerors, and great men. An able man will prefer callings *en evidence* which all men know of and utilise, and he thus becomes immortalised by universal suffrage.

lxviii. *It is better to help with Intelligence than with Memory.*

The more as the latter needs only recollection, the former νοῦς. Many persons omit the *à propos* because it does not occur to them; a friend's advice on such occasions may enable them to see the advantages. 'Tis one of the greatest gifts of mind to be able to offer what is needed at the moment: for want of that many things fail to be performed. Share the light of your intelligence, when you have any, and ask for it when you have it not, the first cautiously, the last anxiously. Give no more than a hint: this *finesse* is especially needful when it touches the interest of him whose attention you awaken. You should give but a taste at first, and then pass on to more when that is not sufficient. If he thinks of No, go in search of Yes. Therein lies the cleverness, for most things are not obtained simply because they are not attempted.

lxix. *Do not give way to every common Impulse.*

He is a great man who never allows himself to be influenced by the impressions of others. Self-reflection is the school of wisdom. To know one's disposition and to allow for it, even going to the other extreme so as to find the *juste milieu* between nature and art. Self-knowledge is the beginning of self-improvement. There be some whose humors are so monstrous that they are always under the influence of one or other of them, and put them in place of their real inclinations. They are torn asunder by such disharmony and get involved in contradictory obligations. Such excesses not only destroy firmness of will; all power of judgment gets lost, desire and knowledge pulling in opposite directions.

lxx. *Know how to Refuse.*

One ought not to give way in everything nor to everybody. To know how to refuse is therefore as important as to know how to consent. This is especially the case with men of position. All depends on the *how*. Some men's No is thought more of than the Yes of others: for a gilded No is more satisfactory than a dry Yes. There are some who always have No on their lips, whereby they make everything distasteful. No always comes first with them, and when sometimes they give way after all, it does them no good on account of the unpleasing herald. Your refusal need not be point-blank: let the disappointment come by degrees. Nor let the refusal be final; that would be to destroy dependence; let some spice of hope remain to soften the rejection. Let politeness compensate and fine words supply the place of deeds. Yes and No are soon said, but give much to think over.

lxxi. *Do not Vacillate.*

Let not your actions be abnormal either from disposition or affectation. An able man is always the same in his best qualities; he gets the credit of trustworthiness. If he changes, he does so for good reason or good consideration. In matters of conduct change is hateful. There are some who are different every day; their intelligence varies, still more their will, and with this their fortune. Yesterday's white is to-day's black: to-day's No was yesterday's Yes. They always give the lie to their own credit and destroy their credit with others.

lxxii. *Be Resolute.*

Bad execution of your designs does less harm than irresolution in forming them. Streams do less harm flowing than when dammed up. There are some men so infirm of purpose that they always require direction from others, and this not on account of any perplexity, for they judge clearly, but from sheer incapacity for action. It needs some skill to find out difficulties, but more to find a way out of them. There are others who are never in straits their clear judgment and determined character it them for the highest callings: their intelligence tells them where to insert the thin end of the wedge, their resolution how to drive it home. They soon get through anything: as soon as they have done with one sphere of action, they are ready for another. Affianced to Fortune, they make themselves sure of success.

lxxiii. *Utilise Slips.*

That is how smart people get out of difficulties. They extricate themselves from the most intricate labyrinth by some witty application of a bright remark. They get out of a serious contention by an airy nothing or by raising a smile. Most of the great leaders are well grounded in this art. When you have to refuse, it is often the polite way to talk of something else. Sometimes it proves the highest understanding not to understand.

lxxiv. *Do not be Unsociable.*

The truest wild beasts live in the most populous places. To be inaccessible is the fault of those who distrust themselves, whose honors change their manners. It is no way of earning people's goodwill by being ill-tempered with them. It is a sight to see one of those unsociable monsters who make a point of being proudly impertinent. Their dependants who have the misfortune to be obliged to speak with them, enter as if prepared for a fight with a tiger armed with patience and with fear. To obtain their post these persons must have ingratiated themselves with everyone, but having once obtained it they seek to indemnify themselves by disobliging all. It is a condition of their position that they should be accessible to all, yet, from pride or spleen, they are so to none. 'Tis a civil way to punish such men by letting them alone, and depriving them of opportunities of improvement by granting them no opportunity of intercourse.

lxxv. *Choose an Heroic Ideal*;

but rather to emulate than to imitate. There are exemplars of greatness, living texts of honor. Let every one have before his mind the chief of his calling not so much to follow him as to spur himself on. Alexander wept not on account of Achilles dead and buried, but over himself, because his fame had not yet spread throughout the world. Nothing arouses ambition so much in the heart as the trumpet-clang of another's fame. The same thing that sharpens envy, nourishes a generous spirit.

lxxvi. *Do not always be Jesting.*

Wisdom is shown in serious matters, and is more appreciated than mere wit. He that is always ready for jests is never ready for serious things. They resemble liars in that men never believe either, always expecting a lie in one, a joke in the other. One never knows when you speak with judgment, which is the same as if you had none. A continual jest soon loses all zest. Many get the repute of being witty, but thereby lose the credit of being sensible. Jest has its little hour, seriousness should have all the rest.

lxxvii. *Be all Things to all Men*

—a discreet Proteus, learned with the learned, saintly with the sainted. It is the great art to gain every one's suffrages; their goodwill gains general agreement. Notice men's moods and adapt yourself to each, genial or serious as the case may be. Follow their lead, glossing over the changes as cunningly as possible. This is an indispensable art for dependent persons. But this *savoir faire* calls for great cleverness. He only will find no difficulty who has a universal genius in his knowledge and universal ingenuity in his wit.

lxxviii. *The Art of undertaking Things.*

Fools rush in through the door; for folly is always bold. The same simplicity which robs them of all attention to precautions deprives them of all sense of shame at failure. But prudence enters with more deliberation. Its forerunners are caution and care; they advance and discover whether you can also advance without danger. Every rush forward is freed from danger by caution, while fortune some-times helps in such cases. Step cautiously where you suspect depth. Sagacity goes cautiously forward while precaution covers the ground. Nowadays there are unsuspected depths in human. intercourse, you must therefore cast the lead at every step.

lxxix. *A Genial Disposition.*

If with moderation 'tis an accomplishment, not a defect. A grain of gaiety seasons all. The greatest men join in the fun at times, and it makes them liked by all. But they should always on such occasions preserve their dignity, nor go beyond the bounds of decorum. Others, again, get themselves out of difficulty quickest by a joke. For there are things you must take in fun, though others perhaps mean them in earnest. You show a sense of placability, which acts as a magnet on all hearts.

lxxx. *Take care to get Information.*

We live by information, not by sight. We exist by faith in others. The ear is the area-gate of truth but the front-door of lies. The truth is generally seen, rarely heard; seldom she comes in elemental purity, especially from afar; there is always some admixture of the moods of those through whom she has passed. The passions tinge her with their colors wherever they touch her, sometimes favorably, sometimes the reverse. She always brings out the disposition, therefore receive her with caution from him that praises, with more caution from him that blames. Pay attention to the intention of the speaker; you should know beforehand on what footing he comes. Let reflection assay falsity and exaggeration.

lxxxi. *Renew your Brilliance.*

'Tis the privilege of the Phœnix. Ability is wont to grow old, and with it fame. The staleness of custom weakens admiration, and a mediocrity that's new often eclipses the highest excellence grown old. Try therefore to be born again in valor, in genius, in fortune, in all.

Display startling novelties, rise afresh like the sun every day. Change too the scene on which you shine, so that your loss may be felt in the old scenes of your triumph, while the novelty of your powers wins you applause in the new.

lxxxii. *Drain Nothing to the Dregs, neither Good nor Ill.*

A sage once reduced all virtue to the golden mean. Push right to the extreme and it becomes wrong: press all the juice from an orange and it becomes bitter. Even in enjoyment never go to extremes. Thought too subtle is dull. If you milk a cow too much you draw blood, not milk.

lxxxiii. *Allow Yourself some venial Fault.*

Some such carelessness is often the greatest recommendation of talent. For envy exercises ostracism, most envenomed when most polite, It counts it to perfection as a failing that it has no faults; for being perfect in all it condemns it in all. It becomes an Argus, all eyes for imperfection: 'tis its only consolation. Blame is like the lightning; it hits the highest. Let Homer nod now and then and affect some negligence in valor or in intellect—not in prudence—so as to disarm malevolence, or at least to prevent its bursting with its own venom. You thus leave your cloak on the horns of Envy in order to save your immortal parts.

lxxxiv. *Make use of your Enemies.*

You should learn to seize things not by the blade, which cuts, but by the handle, which saves you from harm: especially is this the rule with the doings of your enemies. A wise man gets more use from his enemies than a fool from his friends. Their ill-will often levels mountains of difficulties which one would otherwise not face. Many have had their greatness made for them by their enemies. Flattery is more dangerous than hatred, because it covers the stains which the other causes to be wiped out. The wise will turn ill-will into a mirror more faithful than that of kindness. and remove or improve the faults referred to. Caution thrives well when rivalry and ill-will are next-door neighbors.

lxxxv. *Do not play Manille.*

It is a fault of excellence that being so much in use it is liable to abuse. Because all covet it, all are vexed by it. It is a great misfortune to be of use to nobody; scarcely less to be of use to everybody. People who reach this stage lose by gaining, and at last bore those who desired them before. These Manilles wear away all kinds of excellence: losing the earlier esteem of the few, they obtain discredit among the vulgar. The remedy against this extreme is to moderate your brilliance. Be extraordinary in your excellence, if you like, but be ordinary in your display of it. The more light a torch gives, the more it burns away and the nearer 'tis to going out. Show yourself less and you will be rewarded by being esteemed more.

lxxxvi. *Prevent Scandal.*

Many heads go to make the mob, and in each of them are eyes for malice to use and a tongue for detraction to wag. If a single ill report spread, it casts a blemish on your fair fame, and if it clings to you with a nickname, your reputation is in danger. Generally it is some salient defect or ridiculous trait that gives rise to the rumors. At times these are malicious additions of private envy to general distrust. For there are wicked tongues that ruin a great reputation more easily by a witty sneer than by a direct accusation. It is easy to get into bad repute, because it is easy to believe evil of any one: it is not easy to clear yourself. The wise accordingly avoid these mischances, guarding against vulgar scandal with sedulous vigilance. It is far easier to prevent than to rectify.

lxxxvii. *Culture and Elegance.*

Man is born a barbarian, and only raises himself above the beast by culture. Culture therefore makes the man; the more a man, the higher. Thanks to it, Greece could call the rest of the world barbarians. Ignorance is very raw; nothing contributes so much to culture as knowledge. But even knowledge is coarse If without elegance. Not alone must our intelligence be elegant, but our desires, and above all our conversation. Some men are naturally elegant in internal and external qualities, in their thoughts, in their address, in their dress, which is the rind of the soul, and in their talents, which is its fruit. There are others, on the other hand, so *gauche* that everything about them, even their very excellences, is tarnished by an intolerable and barbaric want of neatness.

lxxxviii. *Let your Behavior be Fine and Noble.*

A great man ought not to be little in his behavior. He ought never to pry too minutely into things, least of all in unpleasant matters. For though it is important to know all, it is not necessary to know all about all. One ought to act in such cases with the generosity of a gentleman, conduct worthy of a gallant man. To overlook forms a large part of the work of ruling. Most things must be left unnoticed among relatives and friends, and even among enemies. All superfluity is annoying, especially in things that annoy. To keep hovering around the object or your annoyance is a kind of mania. Generally speaking, every man behaves according to his heart and his understanding.

lxxxix. *Know Yourself*

—in talents and capacity, in judgment and inclination. You cannot master yourself unless you know yourself. There are mirrors for the face but none for the mind. Let careful thought about yourself serve as a substitute.

When the outer image is forgotten, keep the inner one to improve and perfect. Learn the force of your intellect and capacity for affairs, test the force of your courage in order to apply it, and keep your foundations secure and your head clear for everything.

xc. *The Secret of Long Life*

Lead a good life. Two things bring life speedily to an end: folly and immorality. Some lose their life because they have not the intelligence to keep it, others because they have not the will. Just as virtue is its own reward, so is vice its own punishment. He who lives a fast life runs through life in a double sense. A virtuous life never dies. The firmness of the soul is communicated to the body, and a good life is long not only in intention but also in extension.

xci. *Never set to work at anything if you have any doubts of its Prudence.*

A suspicion of failure in the mind of the doer is proof positive of it in that of the onlooker, especially if he is a rival. If in the heat of action your judgment feels scruples, it will afterwards in cool reflection condemn it as a piece of folly. Action is dangerous where prudence is in doubt: better leave such things alone. Wisdom does not trust to probabilities; it always marches in the mid-day light of reason. How can an enterprise succeed which the judgment condemns as soon as conceived? And if resolutions passed *nem. con.* by inner court often turn out unfortunately, what can we expect of those undertaken by a doubting reason and a vacillating judgment?

xcii. *Transcendant Wisdom.*

I mean in everything. The first and highest rule of all deed and speech, the more necessary to be followed the higher and more numerous our posts, is: an ounce of wisdom is worth more than tons of cleverness. It is the only sure way, though it may not gain so much applause. The reputation of wisdom is the last triumph of fame. It is enough if you satisfy the wise, for their judgment is the touchstone of true success.

xciii. *Versatility.*

A man of many excellences equals many men. By imparting his own enjoyment of life to his circle he enriches their life. Variety in excellences is the delight of life. It is a great art to profit by all that is good, and since Nature has made man in his highest development an abstract of herself, so let Art create in him a true microcosm by training his taste and intellect.

xciv. *Keep the extent of your Abilities unknown.*

The wise man does not allow his knowledge and abilities to be sounded to the bottom, if he desires to be honored by all. He allows you to know them but not to comprehend them. No one must know the extent of his abilities, lest he be disappointed. No one ever has an opportunity of fathoming him entirely. For guesses and doubts about the extent of his talents arouse more veneration than accurate knowledge of them, be they ever so great.

xcv. *Keep Expectation alive.*

Keep stirring it up. Let much promise more, and great deeds herald greater. Do not rest your whole fortune on a single cast of the die. It requires great skill to moderate your forces so as to keep expectation from being dissipated.

xcvi. *The highest Discretion.*

It is the throne of reason, the foundation of prudence: by its means success is gained at little cost. It is a gift from above, and should be prayed for as the first and best quality. 'Tis the main piece of the panoply, and so important that its absence makes a man imperfect, whereas with other qualities it is merely a question of more or less. All the actions of life depend on its application; all require its assistance, for everything needs intelligence. Discretion consists in a natural tendency to the most rational course, combined with a liking for the surest.

xcvii. *Obtain and preserve a Reputation.*

It is the usufruct of fame. It is expensive to obtain a reputation, for it only attaches to distinguished abilities, which are as rare as mediocrities are common. Once obtained, it is easily preserved. It confers many an obligation, but it does more. When it is owing to elevated powers or lofty spheres of action, it rises to a kind of veneration and yields a sort of majesty. But it is only a well-founded reputation that lasts permanently.

xcviii. *Write your Intentions in Cypher.*

The passions are the gates of the soul. The most practical knowledge consists in disguising them. He that plays with cards exposed runs a risk of losing the stakes. The reserve of caution should combat the curiosity of inquirers: adopt the policy of the cuttlefish. Do not even let your tastes be known, lest others utilise them either by running counter to them or by flattering them.

xcix. *Reality and Appearance.*

Things pass for what they seem, not for what they are. Few see inside; many take to the outside. It is not enough to be right, if right seem false and ill.

c. *A Man without Illusions, a wise Christian, a philosophic Courtier.*

Be all these, not merely seem to be them, still less affect to be them. Philosophy is nowadays discredited, but yet it was always the chiefest concern of the wise. The art of thinking has lost all its former repute. Seneca introduced it at Rome: it went to court for some time, but now it is considered out of place there. And yet the discovery of deceit was always thought the true nourishment of a thoughtful mind, the true delight of a virtuous soul.

ci. *One half of the World laughs at the other, and Fools are they all.*

Everything is good or everything is bad according to the votes they gain. What one pursues another persecutes. He is an in-sufferable ass that would regulate everything according to his ideas. Excellences do not depend on a single man's pleasure. So many men, so many tastes, all different. There is no defect which is not affected by some, nor need we lose heart if things please not some, for others will appreciate them. Nor need their applause turn our head, for there will surely be others to condemn. The real test of praise is the approbation of famous men and of experts in the matter. You should aim to be independent of any one vote, of any one fashion, of any one century.

cii. *Be able to stomach big slices of Luck.*

In the body of wisdom not the least important organ is a big stomach, for great capacity implies great parts. Big bits of luck do not embarrass one who can digest still bigger ones. What is a surfeit for one may be hunger for another. Many are troubled as it were with weak digestion, owing to their small capacity being neither born nor trained for great employment. Their actions turn sour, and the humors that arise from their undeserved honors turn their head and they incur great risks in high place: they do not find their proper place, for luck finds no proper place in them. A man of talent therefore should show that he has more room for even greater enterprises, and above all avoid showing signs of a little heart.

ciii. *Let each keep up his Dignity.*

Let each deed of a man in its degree, though he be not a king, be worthy of a prince, and let his action be princely within due limits. Sublime in action, lofty in thought, in all things like a king, at least in merit if not in might. For true kingship lies in spotless rectitude, and he need not envy greatness who can serve as a model of it. Especially should those near the throne aim at true superiority, and prefer to share the true qualities of royalty rather than take parts in its mere ceremonies, yet without affecting its imperfections but sharing in its true dignity.

civ. *Try your hand at Office.*

It requires varied qualities, and to know which is needed taxes attention and calls for masterly discernment. Some demand courage, others tact. Those that merely require rectitude are the easiest, the most difficult those requiring cleverness. For the former all that is necessary is character; for the latter all one's attention and zeal may not suffice. 'Tis a troublesome business to rule men, still more fools or blockheads: double sense is needed with those who have none. It is intolerable when an office engrosses a man with fixed hours and a settled routine. Those are better that leave a man free to follow his own devices, combining variety with importance, for the change refreshes the mind. The most in repute are those that have least or most distant dependence on others; the worst is that which worries us both here and hereafter.

cv. *Don't be a Bore.*

The man of one business or of one topic is apt to be heavy. Brevity flatters and does better business; it gains by courtesy what it loses by curtness. Good things, when short, are twice as good. The quintessence of the matter is more effective than a whole farrago of details. It is a well-known truth that talkative folk rarely have much sense whether in dealing with the matter itself or its formal treatment. There are that serve more for stumbling-stones than centrepieces, useless lumber in every one's way. The wise avoid being bores, especially to the great, who are fully occupied: it is worse to disturb one of them than all the rest. Well said is soon said.

cvi. *Do not parade your Position.*

To outshine in dignity is more offensive than in personal attractions. To pose as a personage is to be hated: envy is surely enough. The more you seek esteem the less you obtain it, for it depends on the opinion of others. You cannot take it, but must earn and receive it from others. Great positions require an amount of authority sufficient to make them efficient: without it they cannot be adequately filled. Preserve therefore enough dignity to carry on the duties of the office. Do not enforce respect, but try and create it. Those who insist on the dignity of their office, show they have not deserved it, and that it is too much for them. If you wish to be valued, be valued for your talents, not for anything adventitious. Even kings prefer to be honored for their personal qualifications rather than for their station.

cvii. *Show no Self-satisfaction.*

You must neither be discontented with yourself—and that were poor-spirited—nor self-satisfied—and that is folly. Self-satisfaction arises mostly from ignorance: it would be a happy ignorance not without its advantages if it did not injure our credit. Because a man cannot achieve the superlative perfections of others, he contents himself with any mediocre talent of his own. Distrust is wise, and even useful, either to evade mishaps or to afford consolation when they come, for a misfortune cannot surprise a man who has already feared it. Even Homer nods at times, and Alexander fell from his lofty state and out of his illusions. Things depend on many circumstances: what constitutes triumph in one set may cause a defeat in another. In the midst of all incorrigible folly remains the same with empty self-satisfaction, blossoming, flowering, and running all to seed.

cviii. *The Path to Greatness is along with Others.*

Intercourse works well: manners and taste are shared: good sense and even talent grow insensibly. Let the sanguine man then make a comrade of the lymphatic, and so with the other temperaments, so that without any forcing the golden mean is obtained. It is a great art to agree with others. The alternation of contraries beautifies and sustains the world: if it can cause harmony in the physical world, still more can it do so in the moral. Adopt this policy in the choice of friends and defendants; by joining extremes the more effective middle way is found.

cix. *Be not Censorious.*

There are men of gloomy character who regard everything as faulty, not from any evil motive but because it is their nature to. They condemn all: these for what they have done, those for what they will do. This indicates a nature worse than cruel, vile Indeed. They accuse with such exaggeration that they make out of motes beams wherewith to force out the eyes. They are always taskmasters who could turn a paradise into a prison; if passion intervenes they drive matters to the extreme. A noble nature, on the contrary, always knows how to find an excuse for failings, if not in the intention, at least from oversight.

cx. *Do not wait till you are a Sinking Sun.*

'Tis a maxim of the wise to leave things before things leave them. One should be able to snatch a triumph at the end, just as the sun even at its brightest often retires behind a cloud so as not to be seen sinking, and to leave in doubt whether he has sunk or no. Wisely withdraw from the chance of mishaps, lest you have to do so from the reality Do not wait till they turn you the cold shoulder and carry you to the grave, alive in feeling but dead in esteem. Wise trainers put racers to grass before they arouse derision by falling on the course. A beauty should break her mirror early, lest she do so later with open eyes.

cxi. *Have Friends.*

'Tis a second existence. Every friend is good and wise for his friend: among them all everything turns to good. Everyone is as others wish him; that they may wish him well, he must win their hearts and so their tongues. There is no magic like a good turn, and the way to gain friendly feelings is to do friendly acts. The most and best of us depend on others; we have to live either among friends or among enemies. Seek some one every day to be a well-wisher if not a friend; by and by after trial some of these will become intimate.

cxii. *Gain Good-will.*

For thus the first and highest cause foresees and furthers the greatest objects. By gaining their good-will you gain men's good opinion. Some trust so much to merit that they neglect grace, but wise men know that Service Road without a lift from favor is a long way indeed. Good-will facilitates and supplies everything: is supposes gifts or even supplies them, as courage, zeal, knowledge, or even discretion; whereas defects it will not see because it does not search for them. It arises from some common interest, either material, as disposition, nationality, relationship, fatherland, office; or formal, which is of a higher kind of communion, in capacity, obligation, reputation, or merit. The whole difficulty is to gain good-will; to keep it is easy. It has, however, to be sought for, and, when found, to be utilized.

cxiii. *In Prosperity prepare for Adversity.*

It is both wiser and easier to collect winter stores in summer. In prosperity favors are cheap and friends are many. 'Tis well therefore to keep them for more unlucky days, for adversity costs dear and has no helpers. Retain a store of friendly and obliged persons; the day may come when their price will go up. Low minds never have friends; in luck they will not recognize them: in misfortune they will not be recognized by them.

cxiv. *Never Compete.*

Every competition damages the credit: our rivals seize occasion to obscure us so as to out-shine us. Few wage honorable war. Rivalry discloses faults which courtesy would hide. Many have lived in good repute while they had no rivals. The heat of conflict gives life, or even new life, to dead scandals, and digs up long-buried skeletons. Competition begins with belittling, and seeks aid wherever it can, not only where it ought. And when the weapons of abuse do not effect their purpose, as often or mostly happens, our opponents use them for revenge, and use them at least for beating away the dust of oblivion from anything to our discredit. Men of good-will are always at peace; men of good repute and dignity are men of good-will.

cxv. *Get used to the Failings of your Familiars,*

as you do to ugly faces. It is indispensable if they depend on us, or we on them. There are wretched characters with whom one cannot live, nor yet without them. Therefore clever folk get used to them, as to ugly faces, so that they are not obliged to do so suddenly under the pressure of necessity. At first they arouse disgust, but gradually they lose this influence, and reflection provides for disgust or puts up with it.

cxvi. *Only act with Honorable Men.*

You can trust them and they you. Their honor is the best surety of their behavior even in misunderstandings, for they always act having regard to what they are. Hence 'tis better to have a dispute with honorable people than to have a victory over dishonorable ones. You cannot treat with the ruined, for they have no hostages for rectitude. With them there is no true friendship, and their agreements are not binding, however stringent they may appear, because they have no feeling of honor. Never have to do with such men, for if honor does not restrain a man, virtue will not, since honor is the throne of rectitude.

cxvii. *Never talk of Yourself.*

You must either praise yourself, which is vain, or blame yourself, which is little-minded: it ill beseems him that speaks, and ill pleases him that hears. And if you should avoid this in ordinary conversation, how much more in official matters, and above all, in public speaking, where every appearance of unwisdom really is unwise. The same want of tact lies in speaking of a man in his presence, owing to the danger of going to one of two extremes: flattery or censure.

cxviii. *Acquire the Reputation of Courtesy;*

for it is enough to make you liked. Politeness is the main ingredient of culture,—a kind of witchery that wins the regard of all as surely as discourtesy gains their disfavor and opposition; if this latter springs from pride, it is abominable; if from bad breeding, it is despicable. Better too much courtesy than too little, provided it be not the same for all, which degenerates into injustice. Between opponents it is especially due as a proof of valor. It costs little and helps much: everyone is honored who gives honor. Politeness and honor have this advantage, that they remain with him who displays them to others.

cxix. *Avoid becoming Disliked.*

There is no occasion to seek dislike: it comes without seeking quickly enough. There are many who hate of their own accord without knowing the why or the how. Their ill-will outruns our readiness to please. Their ill-nature is more prone to do others harm than their cupidity is eager to gain advantage for themselves. Some manage to be on bad terms with all, because they always either produce or experience vexation of spirit. Once hate has taken root it is, like bad repute, difficult to eradicate. Wise men are feared, the malevolent are abhorred, the arrogant are regarded with disdain, buffoons with contempt, eccentrics with neglect. Therefore pay respect that you may be respected, and know that to be esteemed you must show esteem.

cxx. *Live Practically.*

Even knowledge has to be in the fashion, and where it is not it is wise to affect ignorance. Thought and taste change with the times. Do not be old-fashioned in your ways of thinking, and let your taste be in the modern style. In everything the taste of the many carries the votes; for the time being one must follow it in the hope of leading it to higher things. In the adornment of the body as of the mind adapt yourself to the present, even though the past appear better. But this rule does not apply to kindness, for goodness is for all time. It is neglected nowadays and seems out of date. Truth-speaking, keeping your word, and so too good people, seem to come from the good old times: yet they are liked for all that, but in such a way that even when they all exist they are not in the fashion and are not imitated. What a misfortune for our age that it regards virtue as a stranger and vice as a matter of course! If you are wise, live as you can, if you cannot live as you would. Think more highly of what fate has given you than of what it has denied.

cxxi. *Do not make a Business of what is no Business.*

As some make gossip out of everything, so others business. They always talk big, take everything in earnest, and turn it into a dispute or a secret. Troublesome things must not be taken too seriously if they can be avoided. It is preposterous to take to heart that which you should throw over your shoulders. Much that would be something has become nothing by being left alone, and what was nothing has become of consequence by being made much of. At the outset things can be easily settled, but not afterwards. Often the remedy causes the disease. 'Tis by no means the least of life's rules: to let things alone.

cxxii. *Distinction in Speech and Action.*

By this you gain a position in many places and carry esteem beforehand. It shows itself in everything, in talk, in look, even in gait. It is a great victory to conquer men's hearts: it does not arise from any foolish presumption or pompous talk, but in a becoming tone of authority born of superior talent combined with true merit.

cxxiii. *Avoid Affectation.*

The more merit, the less affectation, which gives a vulgar flavour to all. It is wearisome to others and troublesome to the one affected, for he becomes a martyr to care and tortures himself with attention. The most eminent merits lose most by it, for they appear proud and artificial instead of being the product of nature, and the natural is always more pleasing than the artificial. One always feels sure that the man who affects a virtue has it not. The more pains you take with a thing, the more should you conceal them, so that it may appear to arise spontaneously from your own natural character. Do not, however, in avoiding affectation fall into it by affecting to be unaffected. The sage never seems to know his own merits, for only by not noticing them can you call others' attention to them. He is twice great who has all the perfections in the opinion of all except of himself; he attains applause by two opposite paths.

cxxiv. *Get Yourself missed.*

Few reach such favor with the many; if with the wise 'tis the height of happiness. When one has finished one's work, coldness is the general rule. But there are ways of earning this reward of goodwill. The sure way is to excel in your office and talents: add to this agreeable manner and you reach the point where you become necessary to your office, not your office to you. Some do honor to their post, with others 'tis the other way. It is no great gain if a poor successor makes the predecessor seem good, for this does not imply that the one is missed, but that the other is wished away.

cxxv. *Do not be a Black List.*

It is a sign of having a tarnished name to concern oneself with the ill-fame of others. Some wish to hide their own stains with those of others, or at least wash them away: or they seek consolation therein— 'tis the consolation of fools. They must have bad breath who form the sewers of scandal for the whole town. The more one grubs about in such matters, the more one befouls oneself. There are few without stain somewhere or other, but it is of little known people that the failings are little known. Be careful then to avoid being a registrar of faults. That is to be an abominable thing, a man that lives without a heart.

cxxvi. *Folly consists not in committing Folly, but in not hiding it when committed.*

You should keep your desires sealed up, still more your defects. All go wrong sometimes, but the wise try to hide the errors, but fools boast of them. Reputation depends more on what is hidden than on what is done; if a man does not live chastely, he must live cautiously. The errors of great men are like the eclipses of the greater lights. Even in friendship it is rare to expose one's failings to one's friend. Nay, one should conceal them from oneself if one can. But here one can help with that other great rule of life: learn to forget.

cxxvii. *Grace in Everything.*

'Tis the life of talents, the breath of speech, the soul of action, and the ornament of ornament. Perfections are the adornment of our nature, but this is the adornment of perfection itself. It shows itself even in the thoughts. 'Tis most a gift of nature and owes least to education; it even triumphs over training. It is more than ease, approaches the free and easy, gets over embarrassment, and adds the finishing touch to perfection. Without it beauty is lifeless, graciousness ungraceful: it surpasses valor, discretion, prudence, even majesty it-self. 'Tis a short way to dispatch and an easy escape from embarrassment.

cxxviii. *Highmindedness.*

One of the principal qualifications for a gentleman, for it spurs on to all kinds of nobility. It improves the taste, ennobles the heart, elevates the mind, refines the feelings, and intensifies dignity. It raises him in whom it is found, and at times remedies the bad turns of Fortune, which only raises by striking. It can find full scope in the will when it cannot be exercised in act. Magnanimity, generosity, and all heroic qualities recognize in it their source.

cxxix. *Never complain.*

To complain always brings discredit. Better be a model of self-reliance opposed to the passion of others than an object of their compassion. For it opens the way for the hearer to what we are complaining of, and to disclose one insult forms an excuse for another.

By complaining of past offences we give occasion for future ones, and in seeking aid or counsel we only obtain indifference or contempt. It is much more politic to praise one man's favors, so that others may feel obliged to follow suit. To recount the favors we owe the absent is to demand similar ones from the present, and thus we sell our credit with the one to the other. The shrewd will therefore never publish to the world his failures or his defects, but only those marks of consideration which serve to keep friendship alive and enmity silent.

cxxx. *Do and be seen Doing.*

Things do not pass for what they are but for what they seem. To be of use and to know how to show yourself of use, is to be twice as useful. What is not seen is as if it was not. Even the Right does not receive proper consideration if it does not seem right. The observant are far fewer in number than those who are deceived by appearances. Deceit rules the roast, and things are judged by their jackets, and many things are other than they seem. A good exterior is the best recommendation of the inner perfection.

cxxxi. *Nobility of Feeling.*

There is a certain distinction of the soul, a highmindedness prompting to gallant acts, that gives an air of grace to the whole character. It is not found often, for it presupposes great magnanimity. Its chief characteristic is to speak well of an enemy, and to act even better to-wards him. It shines brightest when a chance comes of revenge: not alone does it let the occasion pass, but it improves it by using a complete victory in order to display unexpected generosity. 'Tis a fine stroke of policy, nay, the very acme of statecraft. It makes no pretence to victory, for it pretends to nothing, and while obtaining its deserts it conceals its merits.

cxxxii. *Revise your Judgments.*

To appeal to an inner Court of Revision makes things safe. Especially when the course of action is not clear, you gain time either to confirm or improve your decision. It affords new grounds for strengthening or corroborating your judgment. And if it is a matter of giving, the gift is the more valued from its being evidently well considered than for being promptly bestowed: long expected is highest prized. And if you have to deny, you gain time to decide how and when to mature the No that it may be made palatable. Besides, after the first heat of desire is passed the repulse of refusal is felt less keenly in cold blood. But especially when men press for a reply is it best to defer it, for as often as not that is only a feint to disarm attention.

cxxxiii. *Better Mad with the rest of the World than Wise alone.*

So say politicians. If all are so, one is no worse off than the rest, whereas solitary wisdom passes for folly. So important is it to sail with the stream. The greatest wisdom often consists in ignorance, or the pretence of it. One has to live with others, and others are mostly ignorant. "To live entirely alone one must be very like a god or quite like a wild beast," but I would turn the aphorism by saying: Better be wise with the many than a fool all alone. There be some too who seek to be original by seeking chimeras.

cxxxiv. *Double your Resources.*

You thereby double your life. One must not depend on one thing or trust to only one resource, however pre-eminent. Everything should be kept double, especially the causes of success, of favor, or of esteem. The moon's mutability transcends everything and gives a limit to all existence, especially of things dependent on human will, the most brittle of all things. To guard against this inconstancy should be the sage's care, and for this the chief rule of life is to keep a double store of good and useful qualities. Thus as Nature gives us in duplicate the most important of our limbs and those most exposed to risk, so Art should deal with the qualities on which we depend for success.

cxxxv. *Do not nourish the Spirit of Contradiction.*

It only proves you foolish or peevish, and prudence should guard against this strenuously. To find difficulties in everything may prove you clever, but such wrangling writes you down a fool. Such folk make a mimic war out of the most pleasant conversation, and in this way act as enemies towards their associates rather than towards those with whom they do not consort. Grit grates most in delicacies, and so does contradiction in amusement. They are both foolish and cruel who yoke together the wild beast and the tame.

cxxxvi. *Post Yourself in the Centre of Things.*

So you feel the pulse of affairs. Many lose their way either in the ramifications of useless discussion or in the brushwood of wearisome verbosity without ever realising the real matter at issue. They go over a single point a hundred times, wearying themselves and others, and yet never touch the all-important centre of affairs. This comes from a confusion of mind from which they cannot extricate themselves. They waste time and patience on matters they should leave alone, and cannot spare them afterwards for what they have left alone.

cxxxvii. *The Sage should be Self-sufficing.*

He that was all in all to himself carried all with him when he carried himself. If a universal friend can represent to us Rome and the rest of the world, let a man be his own universal friend, and then he is in a position to live alone. Whom could such a man want if there is no clearer intellect or finer taste than his own? He would then depend on himself alone, which is the highest happiness and like the Supreme Being. He that can live alone resembles the brute beast in nothing, the sage in much and God in everything.

cxxxviii. *The Art of letting Things alone.*

The more so the wilder the waves of public or of private life. There are hurricanes in human affairs, tempests of passion, when it is wise to retire to a harbor and ride at anchor. Remedies often make diseases worse: in such cases one has to leave them to their natural course and the moral suasion of time. It takes a wise doctor to know when not to prescribe, and at times the greater skill consists in not applying remedies. The proper way to still the storms of the vulgar is to hold your hand and let them calm down of themselves. To give way now is to conquer by and by. A fountain gets muddy with but little stirring up, and does not get clear by our meddling with it but by our leaving it alone. The best remedy for disturbances is to let them run their course, for so they quiet down.

cxxxix. *Recognize unlucky Days.*

They exist: nothing goes well on them; even though the game may be changed the ill-luck remains. Two tries should be enough to tell if one is in luck to-day or not. Everything is in process of change, even the mind, and no one is always wise: chance has something to say, even how to write a good letter. All perfection turns on the time; even beauty has its hours. Even wisdom fails at times by doing too much or too little. To turn out well a thing must be done on its own day. This is why with some everything turns out ill, with others all goes well, even with less trouble. They find everything ready, their wit prompt, their presiding genius favorable, their lucky star in the ascendant. At such times one must seize the occasion and not throw away the slightest chance. But a shrewd person will not decide on the day's luck by a single piece of good or bad fortune, for the one may be only a lucky chance and the other only a slight annoyance.

cxl. *Find the Good in a Thing at once.*

'Tis the advantage of good taste. The bee goes to the honey for her comb, the serpent to the gall for its venom. So with taste: some seek the good, others the ill. There is nothing that has no good in it, especially in books, as giving food for thought. But many have such a scent that amid a thousand excellences they fix upon a single defect, and single it out for blame as if they were scavengers of men's minds and hearts. So they draw up a balance sheet of defects which does more credit to their bad taste than to their intelligence. They lead a sad life, nourishing themselves on bitters and battening on garbage. They have the luckier taste who midst a thousand defects seize upon a single beauty they may have hit upon by chance.

cxli. *Do not listen to Yourself.*

It is no use pleasing yourself if you do not please others, and as a rule general contempt is the punishment for self-satisfaction. The attention you pay to yourself you probably owe to others. To speak and at the same time listen to yourself cannot turn out well. If to talk to oneself when alone is folly, it must be doubly unwise to listen to oneself in the presence of others. It is a weakness of the great to talk with a recurrent "as I was saying" and "eh?" which bewilders their hearers. At every sentence they look for applause or flattery, taxing the patience of the wise. So too the pompous speak with an echo, and as their talk can only totter on with the aid of stilts, at every word they need the support of a stupid "bravo!"

cxlii. *Never from Obstinacy take the Wrong Side because your Opponent has anticipated you in taking the Right One.*

You begin the fight already beaten and must soon take to flight in disgrace. With bad weapons one can never win. It was astute in the opponent to seize the better side first: it would be folly to come lagging after with the worst. Such obstinacy is more dangerous in actions than in words, for action encounters more risk than talk. 'Tis the common failing of the obstinate that they lose the true by contradicting it, and the useful by quarrelling with it. The sage never places himself on the side of passion, but espouses the cause of right, either discovering it first or improving it later. If the enemy is a fool, he will in such a case turn round to follow the opposite and worse way. Thus the only way to drive him from the better course is to take it yourself, for his folly will cause him to desert it, and his obstinacy be punished for so doing.

cxliii. *Never become Paradoxical in order to avoid the Trite.*

Both extremes damage our reputation. Every undertaking which differs from the reasonable approaches foolishness. The paradox is a cheat: it wins applause at first by its novelty and piquancy, but afterwards it becomes discredited when the deceit is fore-seen and its emptiness becomes apparent. It is a species of jugglery, and in matters political would be the ruin of states. Those who cannot or dare not reach great deeds on the direct road of excellence go round by way of Paradox, admired by fools but making wise men true prophets. It argues an unbalanced judgment, and if it is not altogether based on the false, it is certainly founded on the uncertain, and risks the weightier matters of life.

cxliv. *Begin with Another's to end with your Own.*

'Tis a politic means to your end. Even in heavenly matters Christian teachers lay stress on this holy cunning. It is a weighty piece of dissimulation, for the foreseen advantages serve as a lure to influence the other's will. His affair seems to be in train when it is really only leading the way for another's. One should never advance unless under cover, especially where the ground is dangerous. Likewise with persons who always say No at first, it is useful to ward off this blow, because the difficulty of conceding much more does not occur to them when your version is presented to them. This advice belongs to the rule about second thoughts [xiii], which covers the most subtle manœuvres of life.

cxlv. *Do not show your wounded Finger,*

for everything will knock up against it; nor complain about it, for malice always aims where weakness can be injured. It is no use to be vexed: being the butt of the talk will only vex you the more. Ill-will searches for wounds to irritate, aims darts to try the temper, and tries a thousand ways to sting to the quick. The wise never own to being hit, or disclose any evil, whether personal or hereditary. For even Fate sometimes likes to wound us where we are most tender. It always mortifies wounded flesh. Never therefore disclose the source of mortification or of joy, if you wish the one to cease, the other to endure.

cxlvi. *Look into the Interior of Things.*

Things are generally other than they seem, and ignorance that never looks beneath the rind becomes disabused when you show the kernel. Lies always come first, dragging fools along by their irreparable vulgarity. Truth always lags last, limping along on the arm of Time. The wise therefore reserve for it the other half of that power which the common mother has wisely given in duplicate. Deceit is very superficial, and the superficial therefore easily fall into it. Prudence lives retired within its recesses, visited only by sages and wise men.

cxlvii. *Do not be Inaccessible.*

None is so perfect that he does not need at times the advice of others. He is an in-corrigible ass who will never listen to any one. Even the most surpassing intellect should find a place for friendly counsel. Sovereignty itself must learn to lean. There are some that are incorrigible simply because they are inaccessible: they fall to ruin because none dares to extricate them. The highest should have the door open for friendship; it may prove the gate of help. A friend must be free to advise, and even to upbraid, without feeling embarrassed. Our satisfaction in him and our trust in his steadfast faith give him that power. One need not pay respect or give credit to everyone, but in the innermost of his precaution man has a true mirror of a confidant to whom he owes the correction of his errors, and has to thank for it.

cxlviii. *Have the Art of Conversation.*

That is where the real personality shows itself. No act in life requires more attention, though it be the commonest thing in life. You must either lose or gain by it. If it needs care to write a letter which is but a deliberate and written conversation, how much more the ordinary kind in which there is occasion for a prompt display of intelligence? Experts feel the pulse of the soul in the tongue, wherefore the sage said, "Speak, that I may know thee." Some hold that the art of conversation is to be without art—that it should be neat, not gaudy, like the garments. This holds good for talk between friends. But when held with persons to whom one would show respect, it should be more dignified to answer to the dignity of the person addressed. To be appropriate it should adapt itself to the mind and tone of the interlocutor. And do not be a critic of words, or you will be taken for a pedant; nor a taxgatherer of ideas, or men will avoid you, or at least sell their thoughts dear. in conversation discretion is more important than eloquence.

cxlix. *Know how to put off Ills on Others.*

To have a shield against ill-will is a great piece of skill in a ruler. It is not the resort of incapacity, as ill-wishers imagine, but is due to the higher policy of having someone to receive the censure of the disaffected and the punishment of universal detestation. Everything cannot turn out well, nor can everyone be satisfied: it is well therefore, even at the cost of our pride, to have such a scapegoat, such a target for unlucky undertakings.

cl. *Know to get your Price for Things.*

Their intrinsic value is not sufficient; for all do not bite at the kernel or look into the interior. Most go with the crowd, and go because they see others go. It is a great stroke of art to bring things into repute; at times by praising them, for praise arouses desire at times by giving them a striking name, which is very useful for putting things at a premium, provided it is done without affectation. Again, it is generally an inducement to profess to supply only connoisseurs, for all think themselves such, and if not, the sense of want arouses the desire. Never call things easy or common: that makes them depreciated rather than made accessible. All rush after the unusual, which is more appetising both for the taste and for the intelligence.

cli. *Think beforehand.*

To-day for to-morrow, and even for many days hence. The greatest foresight consists in determining beforehand the time of trouble. For the provident there are no mischances and for the careful no narrow escapes. We must not put off thought till we are up to the chin in mire. Mature reflection can get over the most formidable difficulty. The pillow is a silent Sibyl, and it is better to sleep on things beforehand than lie awake about them afterwards. Many act first and then think afterwards—that is, they think less of consequences than of excuses: others think neither before nor after. The whole of life should be one course of thought how not to miss the right path. Rumination and foresight enable one to determine the line of life.

clii. *Never have a Companion who casts you in the Shade.*

The more he does so, the less desirable a companion he is. The more he excels in quality the more in repute: he will always play first fiddle and you second. If you get any consideration, it is only his leavings. The moon shines bright alone among the stars: when the sun rises she becomes either invisible or imperceptible. Never join one that eclipses you, but rather one who sets you in a brighter light. By this means the cunning Fabula in Martial was able to appear beautiful and brilliant, owing to the ugliness and disorder of her companions. But one should as little imperil oneself by an evil companion as pay honor to another at the cost of one's own credit. When you are on the way to fortune associate with the eminent; when arrived, with the mediocre.

cliii. *Beware of entering where there is a great Gap to be filled.*

But if you do it be sure to surpass your predecessor; merely to equal him requires twice his worth. As it is a fine stroke to arrange that our successor shall cause us to be wished back, so it is policy to see that our predecessor does not eclipse us. To fill a great gap is difficult, for the past always seems best, and to equal the predecessor is not enough, since he has the right of first possession. You must therefore possess additional claims to oust the other from his hold on public opinion.

cliv. *Do not Believe, or Like, lightly.*

Maturity of mind is best shown in slow belief. Lying is the usual thing; then let belief be unusual. He that is lightly led away, soon falls into contempt. At the same time there is no necessity to betray your doubts in the good faith of others, for this adds insult to discourtesy, since you make out your informant to be either deceiver or deceived. Nor is this the only evil: want of belief is the mark of the liar, who suffers from two failings: he neither believes nor is believed. Suspension of judgment is prudent in a hearer: the speaker can appeal to his original source of in-formation. There is a similar kind of imprudence in liking too easily, for lies may be told by deeds as well as in words, and this deceit is more dangerous for practical life.

clv. *The Art of getting into a Passion.*

If possible, oppose vulgar importunity with prudent reflection; it will not be difficult for a really prudent man. The first step towards getting into a passion is to announce that you are in a passion. By this means you begin the conflict with command over your temper, for one has to regulate one's passion to the exact point that is necessary and no further. This is the art of arts in falling into and getting out of a rage. You should know how and when best to come to a stop: it is most difficult to halt while running at the double. It is a great proof of wisdom to remain clear-sighted during paroxysms of rage. Every excess of passion is a digression from rational conduct. But by this masterly policy reason will never be transgressed, nor pass the bounds of its own synteresis. To keep control of passion one must hold firm the reins of attention: he who can do so will be the first man "wise on horseback," and probably the last.

clvi. *Select your Friends.*

Only after passing the matriculation of experience and the examination of fortune will they be graduates not alone in affection but in discernment. Though this is the most important thing in life, it is the one least cared for. Intelligence brings friends to some, chance to most. Yet a man is judged by his friends, for there was never agreement between wise men and fools. At the same time, to find pleasure in a man's society is no proof of near friendship: it may come from the pleasantness of his company more than from trust in his capacity. There are some friendships legitimate, others illicit; the latter for pleasure, the former for their fecundity of ideas and motives. Few are the friends of a man's self, most those of his circumstances. The insight of a true friend is more useful than the goodwill of others: therefore gain them by choice, not by chance. A wise friend wards off worries, a foolish one brings them about. But do not wish them too much luck, or you may lose them.

clvii. *Do not make Mistakes about Character.*

That is the worst and yet easiest error. Better be cheated in the price than in the quality of goods. In dealing with men, more than with other things, it is necessary to look within. To know men is different from knowing things. It is profound philosophy to sound the depths of feeling and distinguish traits of character. Men must be studied as deeply as books.

clviii. *Make use of your Friends.*

This requires all the art of discretion. Some are good afar off, some when near. Many are no good at conversation but excellent as correspondents, for distance removes some failings which are unbearable in close proximity to them. Friends are for use even more than for pleasure, for they have the three qualities of the Good, or, as some say, of Being in general: unity, goodness, and truth. For a friend is all in all. Few are worthy to be good friends, and even these become fewer because men do not know how to pick them out. To keep is more important than to make friends. Select those that will wear well; if they are new at first, it is some consolation they will become old. Absolutely the best are those well salted, though they may require soaking in the testing. There is no desert like living without friends. Friendship multiplies the good of life and divides the evil. 'Tis the sole remedy against misfortune, the very ventilation of the soul.

clix. *Put up with Fools.*

The wise are always impatient, for he that increases knowledge increase impatience of folly. Much knowledge is difficult to satisfy. The first great rule of life, according to Epictetus, is to put up with things: he makes that the moiety of wisdom. To put up with all the varieties of folly would need much patience. We often have to put up with most from those on whom we most depend: a useful lesson in self-control. Out of patience comes forth peace, the priceless boon which is the happiness of the world. But let him that bath no power of patience retire within himself, though even there he will have to put up with himself.

clx. *Be careful in Speaking.*

With your rivals from prudence; with others for the sake of appearance. There is always time to add a word, never to withdraw one. Talk as if you were making your will: the fewer words the less litigation. In trivial matters exercise yourself for the more weighty matters of speech. Profound secrecy has some of the lustre of the divine. He who speaks lightly soon falls or fails.

clxi. *Know your pet Faults.*

The most perfect of men has them, and is either wedded to them or has illicit relations with them. They are often faults of intellect, and the greater this is, the greater they are, or at least the more conspicuous. It is not so much that their possessor does not know them: he loves them, which is a double evil: irrational affection for avoidable faults. They are spots on perfection; they displease the onlooker as much as they please the possessor. 'Tis a gallant thing to get clear of them, and so give play to one's other qualities. For all men hit upon such a failing, and on going over your qualifications they make a long stay at this blot, and blacken it as deeply as possible in order to cast your other talents into the shade.

clxii. *How to triumph over Rivals and Detractors.*

It is not enough to despise them, though this is often wise: a gallant bearing is the thing. One cannot praise a man too much who speaks well of them who speak ill of him. There is no more heroic vengeance than that of talents and services which at once conquer and torment the envious. Every success is a further twist of the cord round the neck of the ill-affected, and an enemy's glory is the rival's hell. The envious die not once, but as oft as the envied wins applause. The immortality of his fame is the measure of the other's torture: the one lives in endless honor, the other in endless pain. The clarion of Fame announces immortality to the one and death to the other, the slow death of envy long drawn out.

clxiii. *Never, from Sympathy with the Unfortunate, involve Yourself in his Fate.*

One man's misfortune is another man's luck, for one cannot be lucky without many being unlucky. It is a peculiarity of the unfortunate to arouse people's goodwill who desire to compensate them for the blows of fortune with their useless favor, and it happens that one who was abhorred by all in prosperity is adored by all in adversity. Vengeance on the wing is exchanged for compassion afoot. Yet 'tis to be noticed how fate shuffles the cards. There are men who always consort with the unlucky, and he that yesterday flew high and happy stands to-day miserable at their side. That argues nobility of soul, but not worldly wisdom.

clxiv. *Throw Straws in the Air,*

to find how things will be received, especially those whose reception or success is doubtful. One can thus be assured of its turning out well, and an opportunity is afforded for going on in earnest or withdrawing entirely. By trying men's intentions in this way, the wise man knows on what ground he stands. This is the great rule of foresight in asking, in desiring, and in ruling.

clxv. *Wage War Honorably.*

You may be obliged to wage war, but not to use poisoned arrows. Everyone must needs act as he is, not as others would make him to be. Gallantry in the battle of life wins all men's praise: one should fight so as to conquer, not alone by force but by the way it is used. A mean victory brings no glory, but rather disgrace. Honor always has the upper hand. An honorable man never uses forbidden weapons, such as using a friendship that's ended for the purposes of a hatred just begun: a confidence must never be used for a vengeance. The slightest taint of treason tarnishes the good name. In men of honor the smallest trace of meanness repels: the noble and the ignoble should be miles apart. Be able to boast that if gallantry, generosity, and fidelity were lost in the world men would be able to find them again in your own breast.

clxvi. *Distinguish the Man of Words from the Man of Deeds.*

Discrimination here is as important as in the case of friends, persons, and employments, which have all many varieties. Bad words even without bad deeds are bad enough: good words with bad deeds are worse. One cannot dine off words, which are wind, nor off politeness, which is but polite deceit. To catch birds with a mirror is the ideal snare. It is the vain alone who take their wages in windy words. Words should be the pledges of work, and, like pawn-tickets, have their market price. Trees that bear leaves but not fruit have usually no pith. Know them for what they are, of no use except for shade.

clxvii. *Know how to take your own Part.*

In great crises there is no better companion than a bold heart, and if it becomes weak it must be strengthened from the neighboring parts. Worries die away before a man who asserts himself. One must not surrender to misfortune, or else it would become intolerable. Many men do not help themselves in their troubles, and double their weight by not knowing how to bear them. He that knows himself knows how to strengthen his weakness, and the wise man conquers everything, even the stars in their courses.

clxviii. *Do not indulge in the Eccentricities of Folly.*

Like vain, presumptuous, egotistical, untrustworthy, capricious, obstinate, fanciful, theatrical, whimsical, inquisitive, paradoxical, sectarian people and all kinds of one-sided persons: they are all monstrosities of impertinence. All deformity of mind is more obnoxious than that of the body, because it contravenes a higher beauty. Yet who can assist such a complete confusion of mind? Where self-control is wanting, there is no room for others' guidance. Instead of paying attention to other people's real derision, men of this kind blind themselves with the unfounded assumption of their imaginary applause.

clxix. *Be more careful not to Miss once than to Hit a hundred times.*

No one looks at the blazing sun; all gaze when he is eclipsed. The common talk does not reckon what goes right but what goes wrong. Evil report carries farther than any applause. Many men are not known to the world till they have left it. All the exploits of a man taken together are not enough to wipe out a single small blemish. Avoid therefore falling into error, seeing that ill-will notices every error and no success.

clxx. *In all Things keep Something in Reserve.*

'Tis a sure means of keeping up your importance. A man should not employ all his capacity and power at once and on every occasion. Even in knowledge there should be a rearguard, so that your resources are doubled. One must always have something to resort to when there is fear of a defeat. The reserve is of more importance than the attacking force: for it is distinguished for valor and reputation. Prudence always sets to work with assurance of safety: in this matter the piquant paradox holds good that the half is more than the whole.

clxxi. *Waste not Influence.*

The great as friends are for great occasions. One should not make use of great confidence for little things: for that is to waste a favor. The sheet anchor should be reserved for the last extremity. If you use up the great for little ends what remains afterwards? Nothing is more valuable than a protector, and nothing costs more nowadays than a favor. It can make or unmake a whole world. It can even give sense and take it away. As Nature and Fame are favorable to the wise, so Luck is generally envious of them. It is therefore more important to keep the favor of the mighty than goods and chattels.

clxxii. *Never contend with a Man who has nothing to Lose;*

for thereby you enter into an unequal conflict. The other enters without anxiety; having lost everything, including shame, he has no further loss to fear. He therefore re-sorts to all kinds of insolence. One should never expose a valuable reputation to so terrible a risk, lest what has cost years to gain may be lost in a moment, since a single slight may wipe out much sweat. A man of honor and responsibility has a reputation, because he has much to lose. He balances his own and the other's reputation: he only enters into the contest with the greatest caution, and then goes to work with such circumspection that he gives time to prudence to retire in time and bring his reputation under cover. For even by victory he cannot gain what he has lost by exposing himself to the chances of loss.

clxxiii. *Do not be Glass in Intercourse, still less in Friendship.*

Some break very easily, and thereby show their want of consistency. They attribute to themselves imaginary offences and to others oppressive intentions. Their feelings are even more sensitive than the eye itself, and must not be touched in jest or in earnest. Motes offend them: they need not wait for beams. Those who consort with them must treat them with the greatest delicacy, have regard to their sensitiveness, and watch their demeanor, since the slightest slight arouses their annoyance. They are mostly very egoistic, slaves of their moods, for the sake of which they cast everything aside: they are the worshippers of punctilio. On the other hand, the disposition of the true lover is firm and enduring, so that it may be said that the Arrant is half adamant.

clxxiv. *Do not live in a Hurry.*

To know how to separate things is to know how to enjoy them. Many finish their fortune sooner than their life: they run through pleasures without enjoying them, and would like to go back when they find they have over-leaped the mark. Postilions of life, they increase the ordinary pace of life by the hurry of their own calling. They devour more in one day than they can digest in a whole life-time; they live in advance of pleasures, eat up the years beforehand, and by their hurry get through everything too soon. Even in the search for knowledge there should be moderation, lest we learn things better left unknown. We have more days to live through than pleasures. Be slow in enjoyment, quick at work, for men see work ended with pleasure, pleasure ended with regret.

clxxv. *A Solid Man.*

One who is finds no satisfaction in those that are not. 'Tis a pitiable eminence that is not well founded. Not all are men that seem to be so. Some are sources of deceit; impregnated by chimeras they give birth to impositions. Others are like them so far that they take more pleasure in a lie, because it promises much, than in the truth, because it performs little. But in the end these caprices come to a bad end, for they have no solid foundation. Only Truth can give true reputation: only reality can be of real profit. One deceit needs many others, and so the whole house is built in the air and must soon come to the ground. Unfounded things never reach old age. They promise too much to be much trusted, just as that cannot be true which proves too much.

clxxvi. *Have Knowledge, or know those that have Knowledge.*

Without intelligence, either one's own or another's, true life is impossible. But many do not know that they do not know, and many think they know when they know nothing. Failings of the intelligence are incorrigible, since those who do not know, do not know themselves, and cannot therefore seek what they lack. Many would be wise if they did not think themselves wise. Thus it happens that though the oracles of wisdom are rare, they are rarely used. To seek advice does not lessen greatness or argue incapacity. On the contrary, to ask advice proves you well advised. Take counsel with reason it you do not wish to court defeat.

clxxvii. *Avoid Familiarities in Intercourse.*

Neither use them nor permit them. He that is familiar, loses any superiority his Influence gives him, and so loses respect. The stars keep their brilliance by not making themselves common. The Divine demands decorum. Every familiarity breeds contempt. In human affairs, the more a man shows, the less he has, for in open communication you communicate the failings that reserve might keep under cover. Familiarity is never desirable; with superiors because it is dangerous, with inferiors because it is unbecoming, least of all with the common herd, who become insolent from sheer folly: they mistake favor shown them for need felt of them. Familiarity trenches on vulgarity.

clxxviii. *Trust your Heart,*

especially when it has been proved. Never deny it a hearing. It is a kind of house oracle that often foretells the most important. Many have perished because they feared their own heart, but of what use is it to fear it without finding a better remedy? Many are endowed by Nature with a heart so true that it always warns them of misfortune and wards off its effects. It is unwise to seek evils, unless you seek to conquer them.

clxxix. *Reticence is the Seal of Capacity.*

A breast without a secret is an open letter. Where there is a solid foundation secrets can be kept profound: there are spacious cellars where things of moment may be hid. Reticence springs from self-control, and to control oneself in this is a true triumph. You must pay ransom to each you tell. The security of wisdom consists in temperance in the inner man. The risk that reticence runs lies in the cross-questioning of others, in the use of contradiction to worm out secrets, in the darts of irony: to avoid these the prudent become more reticent than before. What must be done need not be said, and what must be said need not be done.

clxxx. *Never guide the Enemy to what he has to do.*

The fool never does what the wise judge wise, because he does not follow up the suitable means. He that is discreet follows still less a plan laid out, or even carried out, by another. One has to discuss matters from both points of view—turn it over on both sides. Judgments vary; let him that has not decided attend rather to what is possible than what is probable.

clxxxi. *The Truth, but not the whole Truth.*

Nothing demands more caution than the truth: 'tis the lancet of the heart. It requires as much to tell the truth as to conceal it. A single lie destroys a whole reputation for integrity. The deceit is regarded as treason and the deceiver as a traitor, which is worse. Yet not all truths can be spoken: some for our own sake, others for the sake of others.

clxxxii. *A Grain of Boldness in Everything.*

'Tis an important piece of prudence. You must moderate your opinion of others so that you may not think so high of them as to fear them. The imagination should never yield to the heart. Many appear great till you know them personally, and then dealing with them does more to disillusionise than to raise esteem. No one o'ersteps the narrow bounds of humanity: all have their weaknesses either in heart or head. Dignity gives apparent authority, which is rarely accompanied by personal power: for Fortune often redresses the height of office by the inferiority of the holder. The imagination always jumps too soon, and paints things in brighter colors than the real: it thinks things not as they are but as it wishes them to be. Attentive experience disillusionised in the past soon corrects all that. Yet if wisdom should not be timorous, neither should folly be rash. And if self-reliance helps the ignorant, how much more the brave and wise?

clxxxiii. *Do not hold your Views too firmly.*

Every fool is fully convinced, and every one fully persuaded is a fool: the more erroneous his judgment the more firmly he holds it. Even in cases of obvious certainty, it is fine to yield: our reasons for holding the view cannot escape notice, our courtesy in yielding must be the more recognized. Our obstinacy loses more than our victory yields: that is not to champion truth but rather rudeness. There be some heads of iron most difficult to turn: add caprice to obstinacy and the sum is a wearisome fool. Steadfastness should be for the will, not for the mind.

Yet there are exceptions where one would fail twice, owning oneself wrong both in judgment and in the execution of it.

clxxxiv. *Do not be Ceremonious.*

Even in a king affectation in this was renowned for its eccentricity. To be punctilious is to be a bore, yet whole nations have this peculiarity. The garb of folly is woven out of such things. Such folk are worshippers of their own dignity, yet show how little it is justified since they fear that the least thing can destroy it. It is right to demand respect, but not to be considered a master of ceremonies. Yet it is true that a man to do without ceremonies must possess supreme qualities. Neither affect nor despise etiquette: he cannot be great who is great at such little things.

clxxxv. *Never stake your Credit on a single Cast;*

for if it miscarries the damage is irreparable. It may easy happen that a man should fail once, especially at first: circumstances are not always favorable: hence they say, "Every dog has his day." Always connect your second attempt with your first: whether it succeed or fail, the first will redeem the second. Always have resort to better means and appeal to more resources. Things depend on all sorts of chances. That is why the satisfaction of success is so rare.

clxxxvi. *Recognize Faults, however high placed.*

Integrity cannot mistake vice even when clothed in brocade or perchance crowned with gold, but will not be able to hide its character for all that. Slavery does not lose its vileness, however it vaunt the nobility of its lord and master. Vices may stand in high place, but are low for all that. Men can see that many a great man has great faults, yet they do not see that he is not great because of them. The example of the great is so specious that it even glosses over viciousness, till it may so affect those who flatter it that they do not notice that what they gloss over in the great they abominate in the lower classes.

clxxxvii. *Do pleasant Things Yourself, unpleasant Things through Others.*

By the one course you gain goodwill, by the other you avoid hatred. A great man takes more pleasure in doing a favor than in receiving one: it is the privilege of his generous nature. One cannot easily cause pain to another without suffering pain either from sympathy or from remorse. In high place one can only work by means of rewards and punishment, so grant the first yourself, inflict the other through others. Have someone against whom the weapons of discontent, hatred, and slander may be directed. For the rage of the mob is like that of a dog: missing the cause of its pain it turns to bite the whip itself, and though this is not the real culprit, it has to pay the penalty.

clxxxviii. *Be the Bearer of Praise.*

This increases our credit for good taste, since it shows that we have learnt elsewhere to know what is excellent, and hence how to prize it in the present company. It gives material for conversation and for imitation, and encourages praiseworthy exertions. We do homage besides in a very delicate way to the excellences before us. Others do the opposite; they accompany their talk with a sneer, and fancy they flatter those present by belittling the absent. This may serve them with superficial people, who do not notice how cunning it is to speak ill of every one to everyone else. Many pursue the plan of valuing more highly the mediocrities of the day than the most distinguished exploits of the past. Let the cautious penetrate through these subtleties, and let him not be dismayed by the exaggerations of the one or made over-confident by the flatteries of the other; knowing that both act in the same way by different methods, adapting their talk to the company they are in.

clxxxix. *Utilize Another's Wants.*

The greater his wants the greater the turn of the screw. Philosophers say privation is non-existent, statesmen say it is all-embracing, and they are right. Many make ladders to attain their ends out of wants of others. They make use of the opportunity and tantalize the appetite by pointing out the difficulty of satisfaction. The energy of desire promises more than the inertia of possession. The passion of desire increases with every increase of opposition. It is a subtle point to satisfy the desire and yet preserve the dependence.

cxc. *Find Consolation in all Things.*

Even the useless may find it in being immortal. No trouble without compensation. Fools are held to be lucky, and the good-luck of the ugly is proverbial. Be worth little and you will live long: it is the cracked glass that never gets broken, but worries one with its durability. It seems that Fortune envies the great, so it equalises things by giving long life to the use-less, a short one to the important. Those who bear the burden come soon to grief, while those who are of no importance live on and on: in one case it appears so, in the other it is so. The unlucky thinks he has been for-gotten by both Death and Fortune.

cxci. *Do not take Payment in Politeness*;

for it is a kind of fraud. Some do not need the herbs of Thessaly for their magic, for they can enchant fools by the grace of their salute. Theirs is the Bank of Elegance, and they pay with the wind of fine words. To promise everything is to promise nothing: promises are the pitfalls of fools. The true courtesy is performance of duty: the spurious and especially the useless is deceit. It is not respect but rather a means to power. Obeisance is paid not to the man but to his means, and compliments are offered not to the qualities that are recognized but to the advantages that are desired.

cxcii. *Peaceful Life, a long Life.*

To live, let live. Peacemakers not only live: they rule life. Hear, see, and be silent. A day without dispute brings sleep without dreams. Long life and a pleasant one is life enough for two: that is the fruit of peace. He has all that makes nothing of what is nothing to him. There is no greater perversity than to take everything to heart. There is equal folly in troubling our heart about what does not concern us and in not taking to heart what does.

cxciii. *Watch him that begins with Another's to end with his own.*

Watchfulness is the only guard against cunning. Be intent on his intentions. Many succeed in making others do their own affairs, and unless you possess the key to their motives you may at any moment be forced to take their chestnuts out of the fire to the damage of your own fingers.

cxciv. *Have reasonable Views of Yourself and of your Affairs,*

especially in the beginning of life. Everyone has a high opinion of himself, especially those who have least ground for it. Every one dreams of his good-luck and thinks himself a wonder. Hope gives rise to extravagant promises which experience does not fulfill. Such idle imaginations merely serve as a well-spring of annoyance when disillusion comes with the true reality. The wise man anticipates such errors: he may always hope for the best. but he always expects the worst, so as to receive what comes with equanimity. True, It is wise to aim high so as to hit your mark, but not so high that you miss your mission at the very beginning of life. This correction of the ideas is necessary, because before experience comes expectation is sure to soar too high. The best panacea against folly is prudence. If a man knows the true sphere of his activity and position, the can reconcile his ideals with reality.

cxcv. *Know how to Appreciate.*

There is none who cannot teach somebody something, and there is none so excellent but he is excelled. To know how to make use of everyone is useful knowledge. Wise men appreciate all men, for they see the good in each and know how hard it is to make anything good. Fools depreciate all men, not recognizing the good and selecting the bad.

cxcvi. *Know your ruling Star.*

None so helpless as not to have one; if he is unlucky, that is because he does not know it. Some stand high in the favor of princes and potentates without knowing why or wherefore, except that good luck itself has granted them favor on easy terms, merely requiring them to aid it with a little exertion. Others find favor with the wise. One man is better received by one nation than by another, or is more welcome in one city than in another. He finds more luck in one office or position than another, and all this though his qualifications are equal or even identical. Luck shuffles the cards how and when she will. Let each man know his luck as well as his talents, for on this depends whether he loses or wins. Follow your guiding star and help it without mistaking any other for it, for that would be to miss the North, though its neighbor (the polestar) calls us to it with a voice of thunder.

cxcvii. *Do not carry Fools on your Back.*

He that does not know a fool when he sees him is one himself: still more he that knows him but will not keep clear of him. They are dangerous company and ruinous confidants. Even though their own caution and others' care keeps them in bounds for a time, still at length they are sure to do or to say some foolishness which is all the greater for being kept so long in stock. They cannot help another's credit who have none of their own. They are most unlucky, which is the Nemesis of fools, and they have to pay for one thing or the other. There is only one thing which is not so bad about them, and this is that though they can be of no use to the wise, they can be of much use to them as signposts or as warnings.

cxcviii. *Know how to transplant Yourself.*

There are nations with whom one must cross their borders to make one's value felt, especially in great posts. Their native land is always a stepmother to great talents: envy flourishes there on its native soil, and they remember one's small beginnings rather than the greatness one has reached. A needle is appreciated that comes from one end of the world to the other, and a piece of painted glass might outvie the diamond in value if it comes from afar. Everything foreign is respected, partly because it comes from afar, partly because It is ready made and perfect. We have seen persons once the laughing-stock of their village and now the wonder of the whole world, honored by their fellow-countrymen and by the foreigners [among whom they dwell]; by the latter because they come from afar, by the former because they are seen from afar. The statue on the altar is never reverenced by him who knew it as a trunk in the garden.

cxcix. *To find a proper Place by Merit, not by Presumption.*

The true road to respect is through merit, and if industry accompany merit the path becomes shorter. Integrity alone is not sufficient, push and insistence is degrading, for things arrive by that means so besprinkled with dust that the discredit destroys reputation. The true way is the middle one, half-way between de-serving a place and pushing oneself into it.

cc. *Leave Something to wish for,*

so as not to be miserable from very happiness. The body must respire and the soul aspire. If one possessed all, all would be disillusion and discontent. Even in knowledge there should be always something left to know in order to arouse curiosity and excite hope. Surfeits of happiness are fatal. In giving assistance it is a piece of policy not to satisfy entirely. If there is nothing left to desire, there is everything to fear, an unhappy state of happiness. When desire dies, fear is born.

cci. *They are all Fools who seem so besides half the rest.*

Folly arose with the world, and if there be any wisdom it is folly compared with the divine. But the greatest fool is he who thinks he is not one and all others are. To be wise It is not enough to seem wise, least of all to oneself. He knows who does not think that he knows, and he does not see who does not see that others see. Though all the world is full of fools, there is none that thinks himself one, or even suspects the fact.

ccii. *Words and Deeds make the Perfect Man.*

One should speak well and act honorably: the one is an excellence of the head, the other of the heart, and both arise from nobility of soul. Words are the shadows of deeds; the former are feminine, the latter masculine. It is more important to be renowned than to convey renown. Speech is easy, action hard. Actions are the stuff of life, words its frippery. Eminent deeds endure, striking words pass away. Actions are the fruit of thought; if this is wise, they are effective.

cciii. *Know the great Men of your Age.*

They are not many. There is one Phœnix in the whole world, one great general, one perfect orator, one true philosopher in a century, a really illustrious king in several. Mediocrities are as numerous as they are worth-less: eminent greatness is rare in every respect, since it needs complete perfection, and the higher the species the more difficult is the highest rank in it. Many have claimed the title "Great," like Cæsar and Alexander, but in vain, for without great deeds the title is a mere breath of air. There have been few Senecas, and fame records but one Apelles.

cciv. *Attempt easy Tasks as if they were difficult,*
and difficult as if they were easy.

In the one case that confidence may not fall asleep, in the other that it may not be dismayed. For a thing to remain undone nothing more is needed than to think it done. On the other hand, patient industry overcomes impossibilities. Great undertakings are not to be brooded over, lest their difficulty when seen causes despair.

ccv. *Know how to play the Card of Contempt.*

It is a shrewd way of getting things you want, by affecting to depreciate them: generally they are not to be had when sought for, but fall into one's hands when one is not looking for them. As all mundane things are but shadows of the things eternal, they share with shadows this quality, that they flee from him who follows them and follow him that flees from them. Contempt is besides the most subtle form of revenge. It is a fixed rule with the wise never to defend themselves with the pen. For such defense always leaves a stain, and does more to glorify one's opponent than to punish his offence. It is a trick of the worthless to stand forth as opponents of great men, so as to win notoriety by a roundabout way, which they would never do by the straight road of merit. There are many we would not have heard of if their eminent opponents had not taken notice of them. There is no revenge like oblivion, through which they are buried in the dust of their unworthiness. Audacious persons hope to make themselves eternally famous by setting fire to one of the wonders of the world and of the ages. The art of reproving scandal is to take no notice of it, to combat it damages our own case; even if credited it causes discredit, and is a source of satisfaction to our opponent, for this shadow of a stain dulls the luster of our fame even if it cannot altogether deaden it.

ccvi. *Know that there are vulgar Natures everywhere,*

even in Corinth itself, even in the highest families. Every one may try the experiment within his own gates. But there is also such a thing as vulgar opposition to vulgarity, which is worse. This special kind shares all the qualities of the common kind, just as bits of a broken glass: but this kind is still more pernicious; it speaks folly, blames impertinently, is a disciple of ignorance, a patron of folly, and past master of scandal; you need not notice what it says, still less what it thinks. It is important to know vulgarity in order to avoid it, whether it is subjective or objective. For all folly is vulgarity, and the vulgar consist of fools.

ccvii. *Be Moderate.*

One has to consider the chance of a mischance. The impulses of the passions cause prudence to slip, and there is the risk of ruin. A moment of wrath or of pleasure carries you on farther than many hours of calm, and often a short diversion may put a whole life to shame. The cunning of others uses such moments of temptation to search the recesses of the mind: they use such thumbscrews as are wont to test the best caution. Moderation serves as a counterplot, especially in sudden emergencies. Much thought is needed to prevent a passion taking the bit in the teeth, and he is doubly wise who is wise on horseback. He who knows the danger may with care pursue his journey. Light as a word may appear to him who throws it out, it may import much to him that hears it and ponders on it.

ccviii. *Do not die of the Fools' Disease.*

The wise generally die after they have lost their reason: fools before they have found it. To die of the fools' disease is to die of too much thought. Some die because they think and feel too much: others live because they do not think and feel: these are fools because they do not die of sorrow, the others because they do. A fool is he that dies of too much knowledge: thus some die because they are too knowing, others because they are not knowing enough. Yet though many die like fools, few die fools.

ccix. *Keep Yourself free from common Follies.*

This is a special stroke of policy. They are of special power because they are general, so that many who would not be led away by any individual folly cannot escape the universal failing. Among these are to be counted the common prejudice that any one is satisfied with his fortune, however great, or unsatisfied with his intellect, however poor it is. Or again, that each, being discontented with his own lot, envies that of others; or further, that persons of to-day praise the things of yesterday, and those here the things there. Everything past seems best and everything distant is more valued. He is as great a fool that laughs at all as he that weeps at all.

ccx. *Know how to play the Card of Truth.*

'Tis dangerous, yet a good man cannot avoid speaking it. But great skill is needed here: the most expert doctors of the soul pay great attention to the means of sweetening the pill of truth. For when it deals with the destroying of illusion it is the quintessence of bitterness. A pleasant manner has here an opportunity for a display of skill: with the same truth it can flatter one and fell another to the ground. Matters of to-day should be treated as if they were long past. For those who can understand a word is sufficient, and if it does not suffice, it is a case for silence. Princes must not be cured with bitter draughts; it is therefore desirable in their case to gild the pill of disillusion.

ccxi. *In Heaven all is bliss:*

in Hell all misery. On earth, between the two, both one thing and the other. We stand between the two extremes, and therefore share both. Fate varies: all is not good luck nor all mischance. This world is merely zero: by itself it is of no value, but with Heaven in Front of it, it means much. Indifference at its ups and downs is prudent, nor is there any novelty for the wise. Our life gets as complicated as a comedy as it goes on, but the complications get gradually resolved: see that the curtain comes down on a good *dénoûment*.

ccxii. *Keep to Yourself the final Touches of your Art.*

This is a maxim of the great masters who pride themselves on this subtlety in teaching their pupils: one must always remain superior, remain master. One must teach an art artfully. The source of knowledge need not be pointed out no more than that of giving. By this means a man preserves the respect and the dependence of others. In amusing and teaching you must keep to the rule: keep up expectation and advance in perfection. To keep a reserve is a great rule for life and for success, especially for those in high place.

ccxiii. *Know how to Contradict.*

A chief means of finding things out—to embarrass others without being embarrassed. The true thumbscrew, it brings the passions into play. Tepid incredulity acts as an emetic on secrets. It is the key to a locked-up breast, and with great subtlety makes a double trial of both mind and will. A sly depreciation of another's mysterious word scents out the profoundest secrets; some sweet bait brings them into the mouth till they fall from the tongue and are caught in the net of astute deceit. By reserving your attention the other becomes less attentive, and lets his thoughts appear while otherwise his heart were inscrutable. An affected doubt is the subtlest picklock that curiosity can use to find out what it wants to know. Also in learning it is a subtle plan of the pupil to contradict the master, who thereupon takes pains to explain the truth more thoroughly and with more force, so that a moderate contradiction produces complete instruction.

ccxiv. *Do not turn one Blunder into two.*

It is quite usual to commit four others in order to remedy one, or to excuse one piece of impertinence by still another. Folly is either related to, or identical with the family of Lies, for in both cases it needs many to support one. The worst of a bad case is having to fight it, and worse than the ill itself is not being able to conceal it. The annuity of one failing serves to support many others. A wise man may make one slip but never two, and that only in running, not while standing still.

ccxv. *Watch him that acts on Second Thoughts.*

It is a device of business men to put the opponent off his guard before attacking him, and thus to conquer by being defeated: they dissemble their desire so as to attain it. They put themselves second so as to come out first in the final spurt. This method rarely fails if it is not noticed. Let therefore the attention never sleep when the intention is so wide awake. And if the other puts himself second so to hide his plan, put yourself first to discover it. Prudence can discern the artifices which such a man uses, and notices the pretexts he puts forward to gain his ends. He aims at one thing to get another: then he turns round smartly and fires straight at his target. It is well to know what you grant him, and at times it is desirable to give him to understand that you understand.

ccxvi. *Be Expressive.*

This depends not only on the clearness but also on the vivacity of your thoughts. Some have an easy conception but a hard labor, for without clearness the children of the mind, thoughts and judgments, cannot be brought into the world. Many have a capacity like that of vessels with a large mouth and a small vent. Others again say more than they think.

Resolution for the will, expression for the thought: two great gifts. Plausible minds are applauded: yet confused ones are often venerated just because they are not understood, and at times obscurity is convenient if you wish to avoid vulgarity; yet how shall the audience understand one that connects no definite idea with what he says?

ccxvii. *Neither Love nor Hate, for ever*

Trust the friends of to-day as if they will be enemies to-morrow, and that of the worst kind. As this happens in reality, let it happen in your precaution. Do not put weapons in the hand for deserters from friendship to wage war with. On the other hand, leave the door of reconciliation open for enemies, and if it is also the gate of generosity so much the more safe. The vengeance of long ago is at times the torment of to-day, and the joy over the ill we have done is turned to grief.

ccxviii. *Never act from Obstinacy but from Knowledge.*

All obstinacy is an excrescence of the mind, a grandchild of passion which never did anything right. There are persons who make a war out of everything, real banditti of intercourse. All that they undertake must end in victory; they do not know how to get on in peace. Such men are fatal when they rule and govern, for they make government rebellion, and enemies out of those whom they ought to regard as children. They try to effect everything with strategy and treat it as the fruit of their skill. But when others have recognized their perverse humor all revolt against them and learn to overturn their chimerical plans, and they succeed in nothing but only heap up a mass of troubles, since everything serves to increase their disappointment. They have a head turned and a heart spoilt. Nothing can be done with such monsters except to flee from them, even to the Antipodes, where the savagery is easier to bear than their loathsome nature.

ccxix. *Do not pass for a Hypocrite,*

though such men are indispensable nowadays. Be considered rather prudent than astute. Sincerity in behavior pleases all, though not all can show it in their own affairs. Sincerity should not degenerate into simplicity nor sagacity into cunning. Be rather respected as wise than feared as sly. The open-hearted are loved but deceived. The great art consists in disclosing what is thought to be deceit. In the golden age simplicity flourished, in these days of iron cunning. The reputation of being a man who knows what he has to do is honorable and inspires confidence, but to be considered a hypocrite is deceptive and arouses mistrust.

ccxx. *If you cannot clothe Yourself in Lionskin use Foxpelt.*

To follow the times is to lead them. He that gets what he wants never loses his reputation. Cleverness when force will not do. One way or another, the king's highway of valor or the bypath of cunning. Skill has effected more than force, and astuteness has conquered courage more often than the other way. When you cannot get a thing then is the time to despise it.

ccxxi. *Do not seize Occasions to embarrass Yourself or Others.*

There are some men stumbling-blocks of good manners either for themselves or for others: they are always on the point of some stupidity. You meet with them easily and part from them uneasily. A hundred annoyances a day is nothing to them. Their humor always strokes the wrong way since they contradict all and every. They put on the judgment cap wrong side foremost and thus condemn all. Yet the greatest test of others' patience and prudence are just those who do no good and speak ill of all. There are many monsters in the wide realm of Indecorum.

ccxxii. *Reserve is proof of Prudence.*

The tongue is a wild beast; once let loose it is difficult to chain. It is the pulse of the soul by which wise men judge of its health: by this pulse a careful observer feels every movement of the heart. The worst is that he who should be most reserved is the least. The sage saves himself from worries and embarrassments, and shows his mastery over himself. He goes his way carefully, a Janus for impartiality, an Argus for watchfulness. Truly Momus had better placed the eyes in the hand than the window in the breast.

ccxxiii. *Be not Eccentric,*

neither from affectation nor carelessness. Many have some remarkable and individual quality leading to eccentric actions. These are more defects than excellent differences. And just as some are known for some special ugliness, so these for something repellant in their outward behavior. Such eccentricities simply serve as trademarks through their atrocious singularity: they cause either derision or ill-will.

ccxxiv. *Never take Things against the Grain,*

no matter how they come. Everything has a smooth and a seamy side, and the best weapon wounds if taken by the blade, while the enemy's spear may be our best protection if taken by the staff. Many things cause pain which would cause pleasure if you regarded their advantages. There is a favorable and an unfavorable side to everything, the cleverness consists in finding out the favorable. The same thing looks quite different in another light; look at it therefore on its best side and do not exchange good for evil. Thus it haps that many find joy, many grief, in everything. This remark is a great protection against the frowns of fortune, and a weighty rule of life for all times and all conditions.

ccxxv. *Know your chief Fault.*

There lives none that has not in himself' a counterbalance to his most conspicuous merit: if this be nourished by desire it may grow to be a tyrant. Commence war against it, summoning prudence as your ally, and the first thing to do is the public manifesto, for an evil once known is soon conquered, especially when the one afflicted regards it in the same light as the onlookers. To be master of oneself one should know oneself. If the chief imperfection surrender, the rest will come to an end.

ccxxvi. *Take care to be Obliging.*

Most talk and act, not as they are, but as they are obliged. To persuade people of ill is easy for any, since the ill is easily credited even when at times it is incredible. The best we have depends on the opinion of others. Some are satisfied if they have right on their side, but that is not enough, for it must be assisted by energy. To oblige persons often costs little and helps much. With words you may purchase deeds. In this great house of the world there is no chamber so hid that it may not be wanted one day in the year, and then you would miss it however little is its worth. Every one speaks of a subject according to his feelings.

ccxxvii. *Do not be the Slave of First Impressions.*

Some marry the very first account they hear: all others must live with them as concubines. But as a lie has swift legs, the truth with them can find no lodging. We should neither satisfy our will with the first object nor our mind with the first proposition: for that were superficial. Many are like new casks who keep the scent of the first liquor they hold, be it good or bad. If this superficiality becomes known, it becomes fatal, for it then gives opportunity for cunning mischief; the ill-minded hasten to color the mind of the credulous. Always therefore leave room for a second hearing. Alexander always kept one ear for the other side. Wait for the second or even third edition of news. To be the slave of your impressions argues want of capacity, and is not far from being the slave of your passions.

ccxxviii. *Do not be a Scandal-monger.*

Still less pass for one, for that means to be considered a slanderer. Do not be witty at the cost of others: it is easy but hateful. All men have their revenge on such an one by speaking ill of him, and as they are many and he but one, he is more likely to be overcome than they convinced. Evil should never be our pleasure, and therefore never our theme. The backbiter is always hated, and if now and then one of the great consorts with him, it is less from pleasure in his sneers than from esteem for his insight. He that speaks ill will always hear worse.

ccxxix. *Plan out your Life wisely,*

not as chance will have it, but with prudence and foresight. Without amusements it is wearisome, like a long journey where there are no inns: manifold knowledge gives manifold pleasure. The first day's journey of a noble life should be passed in conversing with the dead: we live to know and to know our-selves: hence true books make us truly men. The second day should be spent with the living, seeing and noticing all the good in the world. Everything is not to be found in a single country. The Universal Father has divided His gifts, and at times has given the richest dower to the ugliest. The third day is entirely for oneself. The last felicity is to be a philosopher.

ccxxx. *Open your Eyes betimes.*

Not all that see have their eyes open, nor do all those see that look. To come up to things too late is more worry than help. Some just begin to see when there is nothing more to see: they pull their houses about their ears before they come to themselves. It is difficult to give sense to those who have no power of will, still more difficult to give energy to those who have no sense. Those who surround them play with them a game of blind man's buff, making them the butts of others, and because they are hard of hearing, they do not open their eyes to see. There are often those who encourage such insensibility on which their very existence depends. Unhappy steed whose rider is blind: it will never grow sleek.

ccxxxi. *Never let Things be seen half-finished.*

They can only be enjoyed when complete. All beginnings are misshapen, and this deformity sticks in the imagination. The recollection of having seen a thing imperfect disturbs our enjoyment of it when completed. To swallow something great at one gulp may disturb the judgment of the separate parts, but satisfies the taste. Till a thing is everything, it is nothing, and while it is in process of being it is still nothing. To see the tastiest dishes prepared arouses rather disgust than appetite. Let each great master take care not to let his work be seen in its embryonic stages: they might take this lesson from Dame Nature, who never brings the child to the light till it is fit to be seen.

ccxxxii. *Have a Touch of the Trader.*

Life should not be all thought: there should be action as well. Very wise folk are generally easily deceived, for while they know out-of-the-way things they do not know the ordinary things of life, which are much more needful. The observation of higher things leaves them no time for things close at hand. Since they know not the very first thing they should know, and what everybody knows so well, they are either considered or thought ignorant by the superficial multitude. Let therefore the prudent take care to have something of the trader about him—enough to prevent him being deceived and so laughed at, Be a man adapted to the daily round, which if not the highest is the most necessary thing in life. Of what use is knowledge if it is not practical, and to know how to live is nowadays the true knowledge.

ccxxxiii. *Let not the proffered Morsel be distasteful;*

otherwise it gives more discomfort than pleasure. Some displease when attempting to oblige, because they take no account of varieties of taste. What is flattery to one is an offence to another, and in attempting to be useful one may become insulting. It often costs more to displease a man than it would have cost to please him: you thereby lose both gift and thanks because you have lost the compass which steers for pleasure. He who knows not another's taste, knows not how to please him. Thus it haps that many insult where they mean to praise, and get soundly punished, and rightly so. Others desire to charm by their conversation, and only succeed in boring by their loquacity.

ccxxxiv. *Never trust your Honor to another,*
unless you have his in Pledge.

Arrange that silence is a mutual advantage; disclosure a danger to both. Where honor is at stake you must act with a partner, so that each must be careful of the other's honor for the sake of his own. Never entrust your honor to another; but if you have, let caution surpass prudence. Let the danger be in common and the risk mutual, so that your partner cannot turn king's evidence.

ccxxxv. *Know how to Ask.*

With some nothing easier: with others nothing so difficult. For there are men who cannot refuse: with them no skill is required. But with others their first word at all times is No; with them great art is required, and with all the propitious moment. Surprise them when in a pleasant mood, when a repast of body or soul has just left them refreshed, if only their shrewdness has not anticipated the cunning of the applicant. The days of joy are the days of favor, for joy overflows from the inner man into the outward creation. It is no use applying when another has been refused, since the objection to a No has just been overcome. Nor is it a good time after sorrow. To oblige a person beforehand is a sure way, unless he is mean.

ccxxxvi. *Make an Obligation beforehand of what*
would have to be a Reward afterwards.

This is a stroke of subtle policy; to grant favors before they are deserved is a proof of being obliging. Favors thus granted beforehand have two great advantages: the promptness of the gift obliges the recipient the more strongly; and the same gift which would afterwards be merely a reward is beforehand an obligation. This is a subtle means of transforming obligations, since that which would have forced the superior to reward is changed into one that obliges the one obliged to satisfy the obligation. But this is only suitable for men who have the feeling of obligation, since with men of lower stamp the honorarium paid beforehand acts rather as a bit than as a spur.

ccxxxvii. Never share the Secrets of your Superiors.

You may think you will share pears, but you will only share parings. Many have been ruined by being confidants: they are like sops of bread used as forks, they run the same risk of being eaten up afterwards. It is no favor in a prince to share a secret: it is only a relief. Many break the mirror that reminds them of their ugliness. We do not like seeing those who have seen us as we are: nor is he seen In a favorable light who has seen us in an unfavorable one. None ought to be too much beholden to us, least of all one of the great, unless it be for benefits done him rather than for such favors received from him. Especially dangerous are secrets entrusted to friends. He that communicates his secret to another makes himself that other's slave. With a prince this is an intolerable position which cannot last. He will desire to recover his lost liberty, and to gain it will overturn everything, including right and reason. Accordingly neither tell secrets nor listen to them.

ccxxxviii. Know what is wanting in Yourself.

Many would have been great personages if they had not had something wanting without which they could not rise to the height of perfection. It is remarkable with some that they could be much better if they could he better in something. They do not perhaps take themselves seriously enough to do justice to their great abilities; some are wanting in geniality of disposition, a quality which their entourage soon find the want of, especially if they are in high office. Some are without organizing ability, others lack moderation. In all such cases a careful man may make of habit a second nature.

ccxxxix. Do not be Captious.

It is much more important to be sensible. To know more than is necessary blunts your weapons, for fine points generally bend or break. Common-sense truth is the surest. It is well to know but not to niggle. Lengthy comment leads to disputes. It is much better to have sound sense, which does not wander from the matter in hand.

ccxl. *Make use of Folly.*

The wisest play this card at times, and there are times when the greatest wisdom lies in seeming not to be wise. You need not be unwise, but merely affect unwisdom. To be wise with fools and foolish with the wise were of little use. Speak to each in his own language. He is no fool who affects folly, but he is who suffers from it. Ingenuous folly rather than the pretended is the true foolishness, since cleverness has arrived at such a pitch. To be well liked one must dress in the skin of the simplest of animals.

ccxli. *Put up with Raillery, but do not practise it.*

The first is a form of courtesy, the second may lead to embarrassment. To snarl at play has something of the beast and seems to have more. Audacious raillery is delightful: to stand it proves power. To show oneself annoyed causes the other to be annoyed. Best leave it alone; the surest way not to put on the cap that might fit. The most serious matters have arisen out of jests. Nothing requires more tact and attention. Before you begin to joke know how far the subject of your joke is able to bear it.

ccxlii. *Push Advantages.*

Some put all their strength in the commencement and never carry a thing to a conclusion. They invent but never execute. These be paltering spirits. They obtain no fame, for they sustain no game to the end. Everything stops at a single stop. This arises in some from impatience, which is the failing of the Spaniard, as patience is the virtue of the Belgian. The latter bring things to an end, the former come to an end with things. They sweat away till the obstacle is surmounted, but content themselves with surmounting it: they do not know how to push the victory home. They prove that they can but will not: but this proves always that they cannot, or have no stability. If the undertaking is good, why not finish it? If it is bad, why undertake it? Strike down your quarry, if you are wise; be not content to flush it.

ccxliii. *Do not be too much of a Dove.*

Alternate the cunning of the serpent with the candor of the dove. Nothing is easier than to deceive an honest man. He believes in much who lies in naught; who does no deceit, has much confidence. To be deceived is not always due to stupidity, it may arise from sheer goodness. There are two sets of men who can guard themselves from injury: those who have experienced it at their own cost, and those who have observed it at the cost of others. Prudence should use as much suspicion as subtlety uses snares, and none need be so good as to enable others to do him ill. Combine in yourself the dove and the serpent, not as a monster but as a prodigy.

ccxliv. *Create a feeling of Obligation.*

Some transform favors received into favors bestowed, and seem, or let it be thought, that they are doing a favor when receiving one. There are some so astute that they get honor by asking, and buy their own advantage with applause from others. They manage matters so cleverly that they seem to be doing others a service when receiving one from them. They transpose the order of obligation with extraordinary skill, or at least render it doubtful who has obliged whom. They buy the best by praising it, and make a flattering honor out of the pleasure they express. They oblige by their courtesy, and thus make men beholden for what they themselves should be beholden. In this way they conjugate "to oblige" in the active instead of in the passive voice, thereby proving themselves better politicians than grammarians. This is a subtle piece of *finesse*; a still greater is to perceive it, and to retaliate on such fools' bargains by paying in their own coin, and so coming by your own again.

ccxlv. *Original and out-of-the-way Views*

are signs of superior ability. We do not think much of a man who never contradicts us that is no sign he loves us, but rather that he loves himself. Do not be deceived by flattery, and thereby have to pay for it: rather condemn it. Besides you may take credit for being censured by some, especially if they are those of whom the good speak ill. On the contrary, it should disturb us if our affairs please everyone, for that is a sign that they are of little worth. Perfection is for the few.

ccxlvi. *Never offer Satisfaction unless it is demanded.*

And if they do demand it, it is a kind of crime to give more than necessary. To excuse oneself before there is occasion is to accuse oneself. To draw blood in full health gives the hint to ill-will. An excuse unexpected arouses suspicion from its slumbers. Nor need a shrewd person show himself aware of another's suspicion, which is equivalent to seeking out offence. He had best disarm distrust by the integrity of his conduct.

ccxlvii. *Know a little more, live a little less.*

Some say the opposite. To be at ease is better than to be at business. Nothing really belongs to us but time, which even he has who has nothing else. It is equally unfortunate to waste your precious life in mechanical tasks or in a profusion of important work. Do not heap up occupation and thereby envy: otherwise you complicate life and exhaust your mind. Some wish to apply the same principle to knowledge, but unless one knows one does not truly live.

ccxlviii. *Do not go with the last Speaker.*

There are persons who go by the latest edition, and thereby go to irrational extremes. Their feelings and desires are of wax: the last comer stamps them with his seal and obliterates all previous impressions. These never gain anything, for they lose everything so soon. Every one dyes them with his own color. They are of no use as confidants; they remain children their whole life. Owing to this instability of feeling and volition, they halt along cripples in will and thought, and totter from one side of the road to the other.

ccxlix. *Never begin Life with what should end it.*

Many take their amusement at the beginning, putting off anxiety to the end; but the essential should come first and accessories afterwards if there is room. Others wish to triumph before they have fought. Others again begin with learning things of little consequence and leave studies that would bring them fame and gain to the end of life. Another is just about to make his fortune when he disappears from the scene. Method is essential for knowledge and for life.

ccl. *When to change the Conversation.*

When they talk scandal. With some all goes contrariwise: their No is Yes, and their Yes No. If they speak ill of a thing it is the highest praise. For what they want for them-selves they depreciate to others. To praise a thing is not always to speak well of it, for some, to avoid praising what's good, praise what's bad, and nothing is good for him for whom nothing is bad.

ccli. *Use human Means as if there were no divine ones,*
and divine as if there were no human ones.

A masterly rule: it needs no comment.

cclii. *Neither belong entirely to Yourself nor entirely to Others.*

Both are mean forms of tyranny. To desire to be all for oneself is the same as desiring to have all for oneself. Such persons will not yield a jot or lose a tittle of their comfort. They are rarely beholden, lean on their own luck, and their crutch generally breaks. It is convenient at times to belong to others, that others may belong to us. And he that holds public office is no more nor less than a public slave, or let a man give up both berth and burthen, as the old woman said to Hadrian. On the other hand, others are all for others, which is folly, that always flies to extremes, in this case in a most unfortunate manner. No day, no hour, is their own, but they have so much too much of others that they may be called the slaves of all. This applies even to knowledge, where a man may know everything for others and nothing for himself. A shrewd man knows that others when they seek him do not seek *him*, but their advantage in him and by him.

ccliii. *Do not Explain overmuch.*

Most men do not esteem what they understand, and venerate what they do not see. To be valued things should cost dear: what is not understood becomes overrated. You have to appear wiser and more prudent than he requires with whom you deal, if you desire to give him a high opinion of you: yet in this there should be moderation and no excess. And though with sensible people common sense holds its own, with most men a little elaboration is necessary. Give them no time for blame: occupy them with understanding your drift. Many praise a thing without being able to tell why, if asked. The reason is that they venerate the unknown as a mystery, and praise it because they hear it praised.

ccliv. *Never despise an Evil, however small,*

for they never come alone: they are linked together like pieces of good fortune. Fortune and misfortune generally go to find their fellows. Hence all avoid the unlucky and associate with the fortunate. Even the doves with all their innocence resort to the whitest walls. Everything fails with the unfortunate—himself, his words, and his luck. Do not wake Misfortune when she sleeps. One slip is a little thing: yet some fatal loss may follow it till you do not know where it will end. For just as no happiness is perfect, so no ill-luck is complete. Patience serves with what comes from above; prudence with that from below.

cclv. *Do Good a little at a time, but often.*

One should never give beyond the possibility of return. Who gives much does not give but sells. Nor drain gratitude to the dregs, for when the recipient sees all return is impossible he breaks off correspondence. With many persons it is not necessary to do more than overburden them with favors to lose them altogether: they cannot repay you, and so they retire, preferring rather to be enemies than perpetual debtors. The idol never wishes to see before him the sculptor who shaped him, nor does the benefited wish to see his benefactor always before his eyes. There is a great subtlety in giving what costs little yet is much desired, so that it is esteemed the more.

cclvi. *Go armed against Discourtesy,*

and against perfidy, presumption, and all other kinds of folly. There is much of it in the world, and prudence lies in avoiding a meeting with it. Arm yourself each day before the mirror of attention with the weapons of defense. Thus you will beat down the attacks of folly. Be prepared for the occasion, and do not expose your reputation to vulgar contingencies. Armed with prudence, a man cannot be disarmed by impertinence. The road of human intercourse is difficult, for it is full of ruts which may jolt our credit. Best to take a byway, taking Ulysses as a model of shrewdness. Feigned misunderstanding is of great value in such matters. Aided by politeness it helps us over all, and is often the only way out of difficulties.

cclvii. *Never let Matters come to a Rupture,*

for our reputation always comes injured out of the encounter. Every one may be of importance as an enemy if not as a friend. Few can do us good, almost any can do us harm. In Jove's bosom itself even his eagle never nestles securely from the day he has quarreled with a beetle. Hidden foes use the paw of the declared enemy to stir up the fire, and meanwhile they lie in ambush for such an occasion. Friends provoked become the bitterest of enemies. They cover their own failings with the faults of others. Every one speaks as things seem to him, and things seem as he wishes them to appear. All blame us at the beginning for want of foresight, at the end for lack of patience, at all times for imprudence. If, however, a breach is inevitable, let it be rather excused as a slackening of friendship than by an outburst of wrath: here is a good application of the saying about a good retreat.

cclviii. *Find out someone to share your Troubles.*

You will never be all alone, even in dangers, nor bear all the burden of hate. Some think by their high position to carry off the whole glory of success, and have to bear the whole humiliation of defeat. In this way they have none to excuse them, none to share the blame. Neither fate nor the mob are so bold against two. Hence the wise physician, if he has failed to cure, looks out for someone who, under the name of a consultation, may help him carry out, the corpse. Share weight and woe, for misfortune falls with double force on him that stands alone.

cclix. *Anticipate Injuries and turn them into Favors.*

It is wiser to avoid than to revenge them. It is an uncommon piece of shrewdness to change a rival into a confidant, or transform into guards of honor those who were aiming attacks at us. It helps much to know how to oblige, for he leaves no time for injuries that fills it up with gratitude. That is true *savoir faire* to turn anxieties into pleasures. Try and make a confidential relation out of ill-will itself.

cclx. *We belong to none and none to us, entirely.*

Neither relationship nor friendship nor the most intimate connection is sufficient to effect this. To give one's whole confidence is quite different from giving one's regard. The closest intimacy has its exceptions, without which the laws of friendship would be broken. The friend always keeps one secret to himself, and even the son always hides something from his father. Some things are kept from one that are revealed to another and *vice versâ*. In this way one reveals all and conceals all, by making a distinction among the persons with whom we are connected.

cclxi. *Do not follow up a Folly.*

Many make an obligation out of a blunder, and because they have entered the wrong path think it proves their strength of character to go on in it. Within they regret their error, while outwardly they excuse it. At the beginning of their mistake they were regarded as inattentive, in the end as fools. Neither an unconsidered promise nor a mistaken resolution are really binding. Yet some continue in their folly and prefer to be constant fools.

cclxii. *Be able to Forget.*

It is more a matter of luck than of skill. The things we remember best are those better for-gotten. Memory is not only unruly, leaving us in the lurch when most needed, but stupid as well, putting its nose into places where it is not wanted. In painful things it is active, but neglectful in recalling the pleasurable. Very often the only remedy for the ill is to forget it, and all we forget is the remedy. Nevertheless one should cultivate good habits of memory, for it is capable of making existence a Paradise or an Inferno. The happy are an exception who enjoy innocently their simple happiness.

cclxiii. *Many things of Taste one should not possess oneself.*

One enjoys them better if another's than if one's own. The owner has the good of them the first day, for all the rest of the time they are for others. You take a double enjoyment in other men's property, being without fear of spoiling it and with the pleasure of novelty. Everything tastes better for having been without it: even water from another's well tastes like nectar. Possession not alone hinders enjoyment: it increases annoyance whether you lend or keep. You gain nothing except keeping things for or from others, and by this means gain more enemies than friends.

cclxiv. *Have no careless Days.*

Fate loves to play tricks, and will heap up chances to catch us unawares. Our intelligence, prudence, and courage, even our beauty, must always be ready for trial. For their day of careless trust will be that of their discredit. Care always fails just when it was most wanted. It is thoughtlessness that trips us up into destruction. Accordingly it is a piece of military strategy to put perfection to its trial when unprepared. The days of parade are known and are allowed to pass by, but the day is chosen when least expected so as to put valor to the severest test.

cclxv. *Set those under you difficult Task.*

Many have proved themselves able at once when they had to deal with a difficulty, just as fear of drowning makes a swimmer of a man, In this way many have discovered their own courage, knowledge, or tact, which but for the opportunity would have been for ever buried beneath their want of enterprise. Dangers are the occasions to create a name for oneself; and if a noble mind sees honor at stake, he will do the work of thousands. Queen Isabella the Catholic knew well this rule of life, as well as all the others, and to a shrewd favor of this kind from her the Great Captain won his fame, and many others earned an undying name. By this great art she made great men.

cclxvi. *Do not become Bad from sheer Goodness.*

That is, by never getting into a temper. Such men without feeling are scarcely to be considered men. It does not always arise from laziness, but from sheer inability. To feel strongly on occasion is something personal: birds soon mock at the mawkin. It is a sign of good taste to combine bitter and sweet. All sweets is diet for children and fools. It is very bad to sink into such insensibility out of very goodness.

cclxvii. *Silken Words, sugared Manners.*

Arrows pierce the body, insults the soul. Sweet pastry perfumes the breath. It is a great art in life to know how to sell wind. Most things are paid for in words, and by them you can remove impossibilities. Thus we deal in air, and a royal breath can produce courage and power. Always have your mouth full of sugar to sweeten your words, so that even your ill-wishers enjoy them. To please one must be peaceful.

cclxviii. *The Wise do at once what the Fool does at last.*

Both do the same thing; the only difference lies in the time they do it: the one at the right time, the other at the wrong. Who starts out with his mind topsy-turvy will so continue till the end. He catches by the foot what he ought to knock on the head, he turns right into left, and in all his acts is but a child. There is only one way to get him in the right way, and that is to force him to do what he might have done of his own accord. The wise man, on the other hand, sees at once what must be done sooner or later, so he does it willingly and gains honor thereby,

cclxix. *Make use of the Novelty of your Position;*

for men are valued while they are new. Novelty pleases all because it is uncommon, taste is refreshed, and a brand new mediocrity is thought more of than accustomed excellence. Ability wears away by use and becomes old. However, know that the glory of novelty is short-lived: after four days respect is gone. Accordingly, learn to utilise the first fruits of appreciation, and seize during the rapid passage of applause all that can be put to use. For once the heat of novelty over, the passion cools and the appreciation of novelty is exchanged for satiety at the customary: believe that all has its season, which soon passes.

cclxx. *Do not condemn alone that which pleases all.*

There must be something good in a thing that pleases so many; even if it cannot be explained it is certainly enjoyed. Singularity is always hated, and, when in the wrong, laughed at. You simply destroy respect for your taste rather than do harm to the object of your blame, and are left alone, you and your bad taste. If you cannot find the good in a thing, hide your incapacity and do not damn it straightway. As a general rule bad taste springs from want of knowledge. What all say, is so, or will be so.

cclxxi. *In every Occupation if you know little stick to the safest.*

If you are not respected as subtle, you will be regarded as sure. On the other hand, a man well trained can plunge in and act as he pleases. To know little and yet seek danger is nothing else than to seek ruin. In such a case take stand on the right hand, for what is done cannot be undone. Let little knowledge keep to the king's highway, and in every case, knowing or unknowing, security is shrewder than singularity.

cclxxii. *Sell Things by the Tariff of Courtesy.*

You oblige people most that way. The bid of an interested buyer will never equal the return gift of an honorable recipient of a favor. Courtesy does not really make presents, but really lays men under obligation, and generosity is the great obligation. To a right-minded man nothing costs more dear that what is given him: you sell it him twice and for two prices: one for the value, one for the politeness. At the same time it is true that with vulgar souls generosity is gibberish, for they do not understand the language of good breeding.

cclxxiii. *Comprehend their Dispositions with whom you deal,*

so as to know their intentions. Cause known, effect known, beforehand in the disposition and after in the motive. The melancholy man always foresees misfortunes, the backbiter scandals; having no conception of the good, evil offers itself to them. A man moved by passion always speaks of things differently from what they are; it is his passion speaks, not his reason. Thus each speaks as his feeling or his humor prompts him, and all far from the truth. Learn how to decipher faces and spell out the soul in the features. If a man laughs always, set him down as foolish; if never, as false. Beware of the gossip: he is either a babbler or a spy. Expect little good from the misshapen: they generally take revenge on Nature, and do little honor to her, as she has done little to them. Beauty and folly generally go hand in hand.

cclxxiv. *Be Attractive.*

magnet of your pleasant qualities more to obtain goodwill than good deeds, but apply it to all. Merit is not enough unless supported by grace, which is the sole thing that gives general acceptance, and the most practical means of rule over others. To be in vogue is a matter of luck, yet it can be encouraged by skill, for art can best take root on a soil favored by nature. There goodwill grows and develops into universal favor.

cclxxv. *Join in the Game as far as Decency permits.*

Do not always pose and be a bore: this is a maxim for gallant bearing. You may yield a touch of dignity to gain the general good-will: you may now and then go where most go, yet not beyond the bounds of decorum. He who makes a fool of himself in public will not be regarded as discreet in private life. One may lose more on a day of pleasure than has been gained during a whole life of labor. Still you must not always keep away: to be singular is to condemn all others. Still less act the prude—leave that to its appropriate sex: even religious prudery is ridiculous. Nothing so becomes a man as to be a man: a woman may affect a manly bearing as an excellence, but not *vice versâ*.

cclxxvi. *Know how to renew your Character,*

with the help both of Nature and of Art, Every seven years the disposition changes, they say. Let it be a change for the better and for the nobler in your taste. After the first seven comes reason, with each succeeding luster let a new excellence be added. Observe this change so as to aid it, and hope also for betterment in others. Hence it arises that many change their behavior when they change their position or their occupation. At times the change is not noticed till it reaches the height of maturity. At twenty Man is a Peacock, at thirty a Lion, at forty a Camel, at fifty a Serpent, at sixty a Dog, at seventy an Ape, at eighty nothing at all.

cclxxvii. *Display yourself.*

'Tis the illumination of talents: for each there comes an appropriate moment; use it, for not every day comes a triumph. There are some dashing men who make much show with a little, a whole exhibition with much. If ability to display them is joined to versatile gifts, they are regarded as miraculous. There are whole nations given to display: the

Spanish people take the highest rank in this. Light was the first thing to cause Creation to shine forth. Display fills up much, supplies much, and gives a second existence to things, especially when combined with real excellence. Heaven that grants perfection, provides also the means of display; for one without the other were abortive. Skill is however needed for display. Even excellence depends on circumstances and is not always opportune. Ostentation is out of place when it is out of time. More than any other quality it should be free of any affectation. This is its rock of offence, for it then borders on vanity and so on contempt: it must be moderate to avoid being vulgar, and any excess is despised by the wise. At times it consists in a sort of mute eloquence, a careless display of excellence, for a wise concealment is often the most effective boast, since the very withdrawal from view piques curiosity to the highest. 'Tis a fine subtlety too not to display one's excellence all at one time, but to grant stolen glances at it, more and more as time goes on. Each exploit should be the pledge of a greater, and applause at the first should only die away in expectation of its sequel.

cclxxviii. *Avoid Notoriety in all Things.*

Even excellences become defects if they become notorious. Notoriety arises from singularity, which is always blamed: he that is singular is left severely alone. Even beauty is discredited by coxcombry, which offends by the very notice it attracts. Still more does this apply to discreditable singularities. Yet among the wicked there are some that seek to be known for seeking novelties in vice so as to attain to the fame of infamy. Even in matters of the intellect want of moderation may degenerate into loquacity.

cclxxix. *Do not contradict the Contradicter.*

You have to distinguish whether the contra-diction comes from cunning or from vulgarity. It is not always obstinacy, but may be artfulness. Notice this: for in the first case one may get into difficulties, in the other into danger. Caution is never more needed than against spies. There is no such countercheck to the picklock of the mind as to leave the key of caution in the lock.

cclxxx. *Be Trustworthy.*

Honorable dealing is at an end: trusts are denied: few keep their word: the greater the service, the poorer the reward: that is the way with all the world nowadays. There are whole nations inclined to false dealing: with some treachery has always to be feared, with others breach of promise, with others deceit. Yet this bad behavior of others should rather be a warning to us than an example. The fear is that the sight of such unworthy behavior should override our integrity. But a man of honor should never forget what he is because he sees what others are.

cclxxxi. *Find Favor with Men of Sense.*

The tepid Yes of a remarkable man is worth more than all the applause of the vulgar: you cannot make a meal off the smoke of chaff. The wise speak with understanding and their praise gives permanent satisfaction. The sage Antigonus reduced the theatre of his fame to Zeus alone, and Plato called Aristotle his whole school. Some strive to fill their stomach albeit only with the breath of the mob. Even monarchs have need of authors, and fear their pens more than ugly women the painter's pencil.

cclxxxii. *Make use of Absence to make yourself more esteemed or valued.*

If the accustomed presence diminishes fame, absence augments it. One that is regarded as a lion in his absence may be laughed at when present as the ridiculous result of the parturition of the mountains. Talents get soiled by use, for it is easier to see the exterior rind than the kernel of greatness it encloses. Imagination reaches farther than sight, and disillusion, which ordinarily comes through the ears, also goes out through the ears. He keeps his fame that keeps himself in the centre of public opinion. Even the Phoenix uses its retirement for new adornment and turns absence into desire.

cclxxxiii. *Have the Gift of Discovery.*

It is a proof of the highest genius, yet when was genius without a touch of madness? If discovery be a gift of genius, choice of means is a mark of sound sense. Discovery comes by special grace and very seldom. For many can follow up a thing when found, but to find it first is the gift of the few, and those the first in excellence and in age. Novelty flatters, and if successful gives the possessor double credit. In matters of judgment novelties are dangerous because leading to paradox, in matters of genius they deserve all praise. Yet both equally deserve applause if successful.

cclxxxiv. *Do not be Importunate,*

and so you will not be slighted. Respect yourself if you would have others respect you. Be sooner sparing than lavish with your presence. You will thus become desired and so well received. Never come unasked and only go when sent for. If you undertake a thing of your own accord you get all the blame if it fails, none of the thanks If it succeeds. The importunate is always the butt of blame; and because he thrusts himself in without shame he is thrust out with it.

cclxxxv. *Never die of another's Ill-luck.*

Notice those who stick in the mud, and observe how they call others to their aid so as to console themselves with a companion in misfortune. They seek someone to help them to bear misfortune, and often those who turned the cold shoulder on them in prosperity give them now a helping hand. There is great caution needed in helping the drowning without danger to oneself.

cclxxxvi. *Do not become responsible for all or for everyone,*

otherwise you become a slave and the slave of all. Some are born more fortunate than others: they are born to do good as others to receive it. Freedom is more precious than any gifts for which you may be tempted to give it up. Lay less stress on making many dependent on you than on keeping yourself independent of any. The sole advantage of power is that you can do more good. Above all do not regard responsibility as a favor, for generally it is another's plan to make one dependent on him.

cclxxxvii. *Never act in a Passion.*

If you do, all is lost. You cannot act for yourself if you are not yourself, and passion always drives out reason. In such cases inter-pose a prudent go-between who can only be prudent if he keeps cool. That is why lookers-on see most of the game, because they keep cool. As soon as you notice that you are losing your temper beat a wise retreat. For no sooner is the blood up than it is spilt, and in a few moments occasion may be given for many days' repentance for oneself and complaints of the other party.

cclxxxviii. *Live for the Moment.*

Our acts and thoughts and all must be determined by circumstances. Will when you may, for time and tide wait for no man. Do not live by certain fixed rules, except those that relate to the cardinal virtues. Nor let your will subscribe fixed conditions, for you may have to drink the water to-morrow which you cast away to-day. There be some so absurdly paradoxical that they expect all the circumstances of an action should bend to their eccentric whims and not *vice versâ*. The wise man knows that the very polestar of prudence lies in steering by the wind.

cclxxxix. *Nothing depreciates a Man more than to show he is a Man like other Men.*

The day he is seen to be very human he ceases to be thought divine. Frivolity is the exact opposite of reputation. And as the re-served are held to be more than men, so the frivolous are held to be less. No failing causes such failure of respect. For frivolity is the exact opposite of solid seriousness. A man of levity cannot be a man of weight even when he is old, and age should oblige him to be prudent. Although this blemish is so common it is none the less despised.

ccxc. *'Tis a piece of good Fortune to combine Men's Love and Respect.*

Generally one dare not be liked if one would be respected. Love is more sensitive than hate. Love and honor do not go well together. So that one should aim neither to be much feared nor much loved. Love introduces confidence, and the further this advances, the more respect recedes. Prefer to be loved with respect rather than with passion, for that is a love suitable for many.

ccxci. *Know how to Test.*

The care of the wise must guard against the snare of the wicked. Great judgment is needed to test that of another. It is more important to know the characteristics and properties of persons than those of vegetables and minerals. It is indeed one of the shrewdest things in life. You can tell metals by their ring and men by their voice. Words are proof of integrity, deeds still more. Here one requires extraordinary care, deep observation, subtle discernment, and judicious decision.

ccxcii. *Let your personal Qualities surpass those of your Office.*

Let it not be the other way about. How-ever high the post, the person should be higher. An extensive capacity expands and dilates more and more as his office becomes higher. On the other hand, the narrow-minded will easily lose heart and come to grief with diminished responsibilities and reputation. The great Augustus thought more of being a great man than a great prince. Here a lofty mind finds fit place, and well-grounded confidence finds its opportunity.

ccxciii. *Maturity.*

It is shown in the costume, still more in the customs. Material weight is the sign of a precious metal; moral, of a precious man. Maturity gives finish to his capacity and arouses respect. A composed bearing in a man forms a *façade* to his soul. It does not consist in the insensibility of fools, as frivolity would have it, but in a calm tone of authority. With men of this kind sentences are orations and acts are deeds. Maturity finishes a man off, for each is so far a complete man according as he possesses maturity. On ceasing to be a child a man begins to gain seriousness and authority.

ccxciv. *Be moderate in your Views.*

Every one holds views according to his interest, and imagines he has abundant grounds for them. For with most men judgment has to give way to inclination. It may occur that two may meet with exactly opposite views and yet each thinks to have reason on his side, yet reason is always true to itself and never has two faces. In such a difficulty a prudent man will go to work with care, for his decision of his opponent's view may cast doubt on his own. Place yourself in such a case in the other man's place and then investigate the reasons for his opinion. You will not then condemn him or justify yourself in such a confusing way.

ccxcv. *Do not affect what you have not effected.*

Many claim exploits without the slightest claim. With the greatest coolness they make a mystery of all. Chameleons of applause they afford others a surfeit of laughter. Vanity is always objectionable, here it is despicable. These ants of honor go crawling about filching scraps of exploits. The greater your exploits the less you need affect them: content yourself with doing, leave the talking to others. Give away your deeds but do not sell them. And do not hire venal pens to write down praises in the mud, to the derision of the knowing ones. Aspire rather to be a hero than merely to appear one.

ccxcvi. *Noble Qualities.*

Noble qualities make noblemen: a single one of them is worth more than a multitude of mediocre ones. There was once a man who made all his belongings, even his household utensils, as great as possible. How much more ought a great man see that the qualities of his soul are as great as possible. In God all is eternal and infinite, so in a hero everything should be great and majestic, so that all his deeds, nay, all his words, should he pervaded by a transcendent majesty.

ccxcvii. *Always act as if your Acts were seen.*

He must see all round who sees that men see him or will see him. He knows that walls have ears and that ill deeds rebound back. Even when alone he acts as if the eyes of the whole world were upon him. For as he knows that sooner or later all will be known, so he considers those to be present as witnesses who must afterwards hear of the deed. He that wished the whole world might always see him did not mind that his neighbors could see him over their walls.

ccxcviii. *Three Things go to a Prodigy.*

They are the choicest gifts of Heaven's prodigality—a fertile genius, a profound intellect, a pleasant and refined taste. To think well is good, to think right is better: 'tis the understanding of the good. It will not do for the judgment to reside in the backbone: it would be of more trouble than use. To think aright is the fruit of a reasonable nature. At twenty the will rules; at thirty the intellect; at forty the judgment. There are minds that shine in the dark like the eyes of the lynx, and are most clear where there is most darkness. Others are more adapted for the occasion: they always hit on that which suits the emergency: such a quality produces much and good; a sort of fecund felicity. In the meantime good taste seasons the whole of life.

ccxcix. *Leave off Hungry.*

One ought to remove even the bowl of nectar from the lips. Demand is the measure of value. Even with regard to bodily thirst it is a mark of good taste to slake but not to quench it. Little and good is twice good. The second time comes a great falling off. Surfeit of pleasure was ever dangerous and brings down the ill-will of the Highest Powers. The only way to please is to revive the appetite by the hunger that is left. If you must excite desire, better do it by the impatience of want than by the repletion of enjoyment. Happiness earned gives double joy.

ccc. *In one word, be a Saint.*

So is all said at once. Virtue is the link of all perfections, the centre of all the felicities. She it is that makes a man prudent, discreet, sagacious, cautious, wise, courageous, thoughtful, trustworthy, happy, honored, truthful, and a universal Hero. Three HHH's make a man happy—Health, Holiness, and a Headpiece. Virtue is the sun of the microcosm, and has for hemisphere a good conscience. She is so beautiful that she finds favor with both God and man. Nothing is lovable but virtue, nothing detestable but vice. Virtue alone is serious, all else is but jest. A man's capacity and greatness are to be measured by his virtue and not by his fortune. She alone is all-sufficient. She makes men lovable in life, memorable after death.

Notes

ORIG. refers to the Spanish original, generally from the Barcelona edition of 1734, though I have occasionally referred to the Madrid edition of 1653, and at times used the text of the *Biblioteca de autores epañoles*. This may have occasioned some inconsistencies, especially with regard to accentuation. Schop. refers to Schopenhauer's translation; I have used Grisebach's edition in the Reclam series. M.G.D. is prefixed to quotations from Sir M. Grant Duff's renderings in Fort. Rev., March 1877; Eng. I. and II. refer to the English translations of 1694 and Savage's of 1902 respectively. Page Max.

    ii. *character and intellect*—Orig. "Genio y ingenio"; Schop. "Herz und Kopf"; Eng. I. "Wit and a Genius." The first section of El Discreto has the same title.

       two poles—Orig. "los dos exes del lucimiento de prendas"; M.G.D. "The two axes of the brilliance of our accomplishments."

    iii. *when you explain*; cf. ccliii.

       the Divine way; cf. "It is the glory of God to conceal a thing," Prov. xxv. 2.

    v. *Not he that adorns*—Orig. "No hace el númen el que lo dora sino el que lo adora"; Schop. "Den Götzen macht nicht der Vergolder sondern der Anbeter."

       golden platter—Orig. "del oro al lodo"; lit. from the gold to the mire.

    vi. *A Man*; from *El Discreto*.

ix. *strata*—so Schop. "Schichten"; Orig. "venas donde pasa."

xiii. *Second Thoughts*—Orig. "intencion segunda." The expression and idea is derived from scholastic logic. Terms of second intention, *i.e.* logical technical terms, are doubly abstract, being abstractions of terms of first intention.

    warfare against malice—Orig. "milicia . . . contra la malicia."

xiv. *accident*—Orig. "circumstancia"; again a scholastic term referring to the modes of real being.

    joy in life; cf. Emerson: "Beautiful behavior is the finest of the fine arts."

xv. *make use of the wise*—"Make friends of the wise," said the Seven Sages, *ap*. Stobaeus, *Flor*. iii. 80.

    great thing to know—Orig. "Ay mucho que saber y es poco el vivir"; Schop. takes it as a variant of Hippocrates' maxim, "Art is long," etc., and renders "Das Wissen ist lang, das Leben kurz." See, however, ccxlvii.

xvi. *Knowledge without sense*—"Ciencia sin seso locura doble"; cf. Span. prov. "Ciencia es Locura si buen seso no la cura."

xvii. *impulse*—Orig. "intencion," a reference to xiii, where see Note.

xviii. *Application and Ability*. Galton, *Hereditary Genius*, p. 38, adds zeal or energy.

xix. *Arouse*, etc.; from *El Heroe*, § 16.

xx. *The sage has one advantage*. A favourite maxim of Schopenhauer, quoted by him in his *Wille in d. Natur*, 1836, p. 34, and written on his own copy of *Die Welt als Wille*, obviously applying it to himself. (See Grisebach, *Edita and Inedita*, p. 104.)

xxiii. *soon finds out*—Orig. "para luego y aun repara."

xxv. *Know how*, etc.—Orig. "Been entendedor"; from *El Discreto*. Eng. I. "A good Pryer"; Eng. II. "A good Understanding." The reference is to the Span. prov. "A buen entendedor pocas palabras," *Don Quixote*, ii. cc. 37, 60. Sly uses the later half in *Taming of Shrew* Induction, "Therefore *pocas palabras*, let the world slide, sessa!"

xxvii. *giants are real dwarfs*; cf. Bacon's apophthegm, "Nature did never put her jewels in garrets."

    try the brawn. A slight embellishment. Orig. "para exercitar antes los braços que los ingenios."

xxviii. *great and wise*—Phocion; ap. Plutarch, *Reg. et Imp. Apophthegm*. Phocion, 4.

    chameleons of popularity; cf. ccxcv.

xxix. *Many praise it*; cf. "Probitas laudatur et alget," Juv. *Sat.* i. 74.

xxxi. *Select the Lucky*. Quoted by Addison in Spectator, No. 293.

The Rothschilds are said to act on this principle in their business relations.

Never open; cf. ccliv.

win the odd trick—Orig. merely "hallan con la ventura."

xxxii. *Those make friends*; cf. xl, cxi.

xxxiii. *One is not obliged*; cf. cclx.

xxxv. *All fools*; cf. Stevenson, Kidnapped, c. xiv. as: "I have seen wicked men and fools, a great many of them; and I believe they both got paid in the end; but the fools first."

xxxvi. *favours the bold*; cf. Span. prov. "Al hombre osado la Fortuna lada la mano."

xxxvii. *Keep a Store of Sarcasms*, etc.—Eng. I. and II. "To guess at the meaning of the little Hints that are given us by the bye, and to know how to make the best of them."

xl. From *El Heroe*, § 12.

xliii. From *El Discreto*, "Hombre juizio."

xliv. *for mystery and for use*—Orig. "por lo culto y por lo ventojoso."

xlvii. *One affair*—Orig. has a play upon "empeño" and "despeño," which I have tried to reproduce.

xlviii. *no use boring*—Orig. "No ay en estos donde parar ó todo para."

xlix. From *El Discreto*, c. xviii.

li. *Know how*, etc.; from *El Discreto*, c. ix.

liii. From *El Discreto,* c. xx.

Festina lente—Orig. "Correr á espacio." This is not given in Dielitz' elaborate work on *Wahl-und Denksprüche*, Gorlitz, 1884, so I suspect it was Gracian's version of Augustus' motto, σπεῦδε βραχέως, generally translated *Festina lente*.

lv. *Wait*; from *El Discreto*, c. iii, mainly from the end. It is called an *Allegoria*.

He spake. Charles V. according to *El Discreto*, I.e. Schop. attributes the saying to Philip II.

lvi. *Have Presence of Mind*; from *El Discreto*, c. xiv.

natures of Antiperistasis. The energy aroused by opposition. Johnson gives example from Cowley (M.G.D.) It occurs also in Bacon (*Colors*, vii.) and Browne (*Rel. Med.* II. x.) Macaulay also uses it in his essay on Bacon (Oxford Diet.)

work best in an emergency. So Galton, *Hereditary Genius*, p. 48, who speaks of men "formed to shine under exceptional circumstances," as in the Indian Mutiny.

lvii. *Quickly done*; cf. Herbert, *Jacula Prudentum*, "Good and quickly seldom meet."

lix. *Finish off well*; from *El Discreto*, c. xi.

think of the finish; cf. lxvi.

Few in life—Orig. "Que son raros los deseados."

warmly as—Orig. "lo que se muesta de cumplida con los que vienen de descortes con los que van." M.G.D. "Seldom does fortune conduct a parting guest to the threshold."

lx. *by the helm of state.* So Schop. "Solche Leute verdienen am Staatsruder zu stehen, sei es zur Lenkung oder zum Rath"; Orig. "Merecen estos la asistencia al gobernarle ó para exercicio ó para consejo."

lxi. *To Excel*; from *El Heroe*, p. vi.

lxii. *Use good Instruments.* Chap. iii. of Sir H. Taylor's *The Statesman* is entitled "A Statesman's most pregnant Function lies in the Choice and Use of Instruments."

lxii. *all the blame*; cf. Sir A. Helps's *Essays in Intervals of Business* (Macmillan, 1890), p. 44: "You have to choose persons for whose faults you are to be punished, to whom you are to be the whipping boy."

lxiii. *To be the First*; from *El Heroe*, primor vii.

lxv. *Elevated Taste*; from *El Heroe*, primor v. Eng. II. "The Fine Taste," and so quoted by Addison, Spectator, No. 40n.

lxvi. *See that Things end well*; cf. lix.

A good end gilds. Here the Jesuit speaks.

lxvii. *Prefer Callings "en Evidence"*; from *El Heroe*, primor viii.

kings of Aragon. Gracian was himself an Aragonese.

lxix. *Do not give way*, etc.; from *El Discreto*, c. xiii.

lxxi. *Do not Vacillate*; from *El Discreto*, c. vi.

lxxvi. *Do not always be Jesting*; from *El Discreto*, c. ix.

A continual jest—Orig. "No ay mayor desayre que el continuo donayre."

lxxvii. *Be all Things to all Men.* A touch of Gracian's training as Jesuit.

universal genius—Orig. "varon universal de ingenio en noticias y de genio en gustos" cf. ii.

lxxix. *Join in the fun*; cf. cclxxv.

lxxxi. mediocrity that's new; cf. cclxix.

Change the scene; cf. cxcviii.

lxxxii. *A sage*—Aristotle.

lxxxiii. *leave your cloak*—an image taken from the bull-fight, when the matador allows the bull to rush at his cloak held sideways. Gracian uses the same image in El Criticon, i. 3.

lxxxiv. *blade which cuts*; cf. ccxxiv.

lxxxv. *Manille.* Schop. suggests that this is the Manillio of Hombre, the second best trump (cf. Pope, *Rape of Lock*, iii. 51). But there is a game mentioned by Littré *s.v.*, which is obviously the one referred to by Gracian. In this the nine of diamonds, called Manille, can be made any value the player wishes. Manille thus means a combination of a jack of all Trades and a universal drudge.

lxxxvii. *Culture and Elegance*; from *El Discreto*, c. xvii.

xc. *The Secret*; cf. Fuller, "He lives long who lives well."

   have not the will. So, it is said, negroes and savages die in circumstances where Europeans keep alive simply because they have "the will to live, the competence to be."

xcii. *an ounce of wisdom*—Orig. "Mas vale un grano de cordura que arrobas de sutileza."

xciv. *Keep the extent*, etc.; from *El Heroe*, i.

xcv. *single cast*; cf. clxxxv.

xcvi. *The highest Discretion*—Orig. "la gran sinderesis."

xcviii. *Write your Intentions in Cypher*; from *El Heroe*, ii.

   adopt the policy—Orig. "A linces de discurso gibias de interioridad," I have omitted the lynxes, who have little to do with cuttle-fish (pl. of Sp. *jibia*).

xcix. *Things pass*, etc. A favourite expression of Gracian's; cf. cxxx, cxlvi; cf. also the German proverb, "Was scheint, das gilt."

ci. *What one pursues*—Orig. "Lo que este sigue, el otro persigue."

cii. *find their proper place*—Orig. "No caben en si porque no cabe en ellos la suerte."

cv. *gains by courtesy*—Orig. "gana por lo cortés lo que pierde por lo corta."

cix. *prison*—Orig. "galera," a sort of Bridewell.

cxi. *way to gain friendly feelings*; cf. xxxii, xl.

cxii. *Service Road*—Orig. "Es grande el rodeo de solos los meritos sino se ayudan del favor."

cxix. to be esteemed—Orig. "el que quiere hacer casa hace caso."

cxxii. *Distinction*; from *El Discreto*, c. ii.

cxxvi. *wise try to hide*; cf. Prov. xii. 16 "A fool's vexation is speedily known, but the prudent man concealeth shame."

   live chastely—Orig. "Si no es uno casto, sea cauto"; Schop. turns neatly into Latin, *caute nisi caste*.

   learn to forget; cf. cclxii.

cxxvii. *Grace in Everything*; from *El Heroe*, c. xiii.

cxxix. *Never complain*. "I make it a point never to complain," Mr. Disraeli once said in the House; cf. cxlv.

cxxx. *Even the Right*; cf. xcix.

   things are judged by their rackets—Orig. merely "juzganse las cosas por fuera."

cxxxiii. *Better Mad*, etc.; cf. "In action wisdom goes by majorities," from "The Pilgrim's Scrip" in *Richard Feverel*.

   the aphorism; from Aristotle, *Pol.* i. s; also Heraclitus; cf. Grisebach, Schopenhauer's *Inedita*, 78. Also Bacon, *Essays*.

cxxxvii. *resembles the brute beast.* See preceding note.

cxlvii. *the sage said*—Socrates.

cli. *The pillow is a silent*; quoted by Morley, *Aphorisms*.

clii. *The more he does*—Orig. "Tanto por mas, quanta por menos." Schop. takes it differently: "Sei es dadurch lass er über uns oder class er unter uns stehe."

the cunning *Fabula*—Martial, *Epigr.* viii. 79.

cliii. *Beware of entering.* The great Jewish teacher Hillel gave braver advice: "Where there is no man, dare to be a man" (*Ethics of the Fathers*).

clv. *synteresis*; defined in Doctor and Student, Dial. I. ch. xiv., as: "The natural power of the soul set in the highest part thereof, moving it and stirring it to good and abhorring evil"; cf. Milton, *Common-place Book*, ed. Horwood, § 79; and cf. Saunder, transl. of Schopenhauer, *Aphorismen zur Lebensweisheit*, c. v. § 34.

"*wise on horseback*"; cf. "Nadie es cuerdo á caballo," Span. prov. quoted by Schop.

clvi. *Only after*, etc.—Orig. "Que lo han de ser á examen de la discretion y á prueba de la fortuna, graduados no solo de la voluntad sino del entendimiento."

Intelligence brings friends; cf. Stevenson, Dr. Jekyll: "It is the mark of a modest man to accept his friends ready made at the hands of opportunity."

clviii. *Being in general*; the scholastic maxim running "Quodlibet ens est unum, verum, bonum."

clix. *to put up with things*; ανέχεσθαι και απέχεσθαι, the great Epicurean maxim.

clx. *Be careful in Speaking*; cf. Prov. xxix. 20. "Seest thou a man that is hasty in his words there is more hope of a fool than of him."

clxii. *enough to despise them*; cf. ccv.

who speaks well. "It's poor foolishness," says Adam Bede, "to run down your enemies", cf. Goethe.

clxiv. *Throw Straws*—Orig. "Echar al ayre algunas cosas" merely refers to feigned blows; cf. xiii.

clxv. *poisoned arrows*; rather an embellishment on the orig., which has merely "pero no mala (guerra)."

clxvi. *polite deceit*; cf. cxci.

clxxiii. *Motes offend them*—Orig. "Ofendenla las motas que no son menester yá notas."

the Amant is half adamant. This seems the only way of retaining the "conceit" and jingle of the orig.: "La condition del Amante tiene la mitad de diamante en el durar y en el resistir."

clxxv. *Only Truth—profit*; omitted by Schop.

clxxxii. *A Grain of Boldness*; cf. the opening of Bacon's Essay "Of Boldnesse," and Mrs. Poyser's aphorism, "It's them as take advantage that get advantage in this world, I think."

clxxxvii. *it is the privilege*; cf. cclxxxvi.

> *Have someone*; cf. Bacon, "Of Envy": "The wiser Sort of Great Persons bring in ever upon the Stage some Body upon whom to derive the Envy that would come upon themselves."

cxc. *The unlucky thinks*—Orig. has a play upon the words "suerte" and "muerte."

cxci. *Theirs is the Bank of Elegance*. I have no excuse for this. Orig. simply "Hacen precio con la honra."

cxcii. *no greater perversity*—Orig. "No ay mayor desproposito que tomar lo todo de proposito."

cxciii. *Be intent*—Orig. "Al intendido un buen entendedor."

> *their chestnuts*—Orig. simply "Sacar del fuego el provecho ageno."

cxcvi. *ruling Star*. There are some grounds for believing that great adventurers, like Napoleon, have a subjective star, hallucinatory of course, which appears to them at moments of great excitement; cf. Gallon, *Human Faculty*, 175-176.

cxcviii. *native land a stepmother*; cf. *contra* Galton, *Hered. Gen.*, 360 "As a rule the very ablest men are strongly disinclined to emigrate," and Prov. xxvii. 8.

cc. *Leave Something*; cf. lxxxii, ccxcix.

> *The body must respire*—Orig. "Espira el cuerpo y anhela el espiritu."

ccii. *Former are feminine*; cf. Span. prov. "Palabras hembras son hechos machos." Howell, *Fam. Letters*, quotes the saying as Italian; cf. my edition, p. 270 and *n*. Herbert also gives it in his *Jacula Prudentum*.

> *Eminent deeds endure*. Schop. has characteristically expressed his dissent by annotating his own copy of the *Oráculo* at this point with a pithy "vale el contrario."

cciv. *Attempt easy Tasks as if they were difficult*. Approved by Mr. Morley, *Aphorisms*.

ccxx. *If you cannot*, etc. There may be here a reference to Lysander's saying in Plutarch: "If the lion's skin [of Hercules] is not long enough, we must stitch on to it a fox's skin."

ccxxi. *They are always on the point of some stupidity*—omitted by Schop. *meet with them easily*—Orig. "Encuentranse con gran facilidad y rompen con infelicidad."

ccxxii. *Reserve is proof*; cf. clxxix.

ccxxiii. *more defects*—so Orig. "Que son mas defectos que diferencias."

ccxxiv. *taken by the blade*; cf. lxxxiv.

ccxxv. *Know your chief Fault*; cf. xxxiv.

ccxxvii. *new casks*; cf. the Span. prov. "A la vasija nueva dura el resabio."

ccxxxvii. *share pears*—Orig. "Pensará partir peras y partirá piedras." Schop. "Man glaubt Kirschen mit ihnen zu essen, wird aber nur die steine erhalten."

ccxxxviii. *communicates his secret*; cf. Span. prov. "A quien dizes poridad á esse tu das la liberdad," neither tell secrets nor listen to them—Eng. I. puts it rather neatly: "Tis a maxim for secrets Neither to hear them nor to tell them"; cf. the maxim of the Seven Sages, ap. Stobaeus, Flor. iii. 80: "Tell none a secret."

ccxxxviii. *something wanting*; cf. xxxiv, ccxxv.

ccxl. *Speak to each*; cf. Prov. xxvi. 5, "Answer a fool according to his folly."

ccxlii. *Everything stops*—Orig. "Todo para en parar." Schop. omits.

ccxlvi. *To excuse oneself*—Orig. "El escusarse antes de ocasion es culparse"; cf. Fr. prov. "Qui s'excuse s'accuse."

ccli. *Use human Means*, etc.; cf. "Human wit ought to be exhausted before we presume to invoke Divine interposition" (B. Disraeli, *Tancred*).

cclii. *berth and burthen*—Orig. "Renuncie el cargo con la carga." The story goes that an old woman met Hadrian with a petition. He repulsed her, saying he had no time. "Then give up your berth," retorted the beldam. Hadrian recognized the justice of the rebuke and decided the petition on the spot.

   slaves of all; cf. "Men in great Place are thrice servants" (Bacon, Essay "Of Great Place"). There is something like this in *El Criticon*, i. 7.

ccliii. *Do not Explain overmuch*; cf. "Let the wise be warned against too great readiness of explanation" (G. Eliot, *Middlemarch*).

   do not esteem what they understand; cf.—
      "Was man nicht weiss, das eben brauchte man,
      Und was man weiss kann man nicht brauchen."
                              GOETHE, Faust, Th. I.

   venerate the unknown; cf. "Omne ignotum pro magnifico."

ccliv. *they never come alone*; cf. Span. prov. *ap. Don Quixote*, i. 28, "Un mal llama á otro," and Shakespeare, "When sorrows come, they come not single spies, But in battalions," *Hamlet*, iv. 5.

   Do not wake Misfortune; cf. Span. prov. "Quando la mala Fortuna se duerme, nadie la despierte."

One slip is a little thing; cf. Stevenson, *Dr. Jekyll.*

cclxii. *The things we remember best are those better forgotten.*—quoted by Mr. Morley in *Aphorisms.*

cclxiv. *Have no careless Days.* D'Artagnan acts on this principle in keeping always on guard over the king during journeys. *Vicomte de Bragelonne*, c. xii.

cclxv. *The Great Captain*—Orig. "El gran Capitan," a reference to Gonsalvo de Cordova (1443-1515), who commanded the Spanish land forces against Chas. VIII. in Italy, and received his title "el gran Capitan" July 1496.

cclxvii. *Silken Words.* Parysatis, mother of the younger Cyrus, advised one who was about to have an audience with a king to use words wrapped in fine linen; cf. Paley, *Greek Wit*, i. No. 152.

> *mouth full of sugar*; cf. *contra* Spurgeon's *John Ploughman's Talk*, "Do not be all sugar, or the world will suck you down."

cclxviii. *Wise does at once*; cf. Span. prov. "Lo que hace el loco á la postre, hace sabio al principio (quoted by Trench, *Proverbs*[5], 116).

cclxxi. *Let little knowledge*—Orig. "A poco saber camino real."

cclxxiii. *If a man laughs always*—Orig. "Conosca al que siempre rie por falto y al que nunca por falso."

cclxxvi. *At twenty*; cf. the ages in *Ethics of the Jewish Fathers*, ed. C. Taylor, p. 111; L. Löw, *Die Lebensalter*, p. 22 and *n*.; and Shakespeare in *As You Like It.*

cclxxvii. From *El Discreto*, c. xii.

cclxxix. *comes from cunning*; cf. ccxiii.

cclxxxi. *you cannot make a meal*—Orig. "Porque regueldos de aristas no alientan." Schop. omits.

cclxxxii. *ridiculous result*—Orig. "Ridiculo parto de los mantes," a reference to Horace's "Parturiunt montes, nascetur ridiculus mus."

cclxxxv. *Never die*—Schop. adds to his copy "y mucho menos de necedad y ruindad agena."

cclxxxvi. *you can do more good*; cf. clxxxvii; cf. "Power to doe good is the true and lawfull end of Aspiring" (Bacon, "Of Great Place").

cclxxxviii. *steering by the wind.* The derangement of metaphors is mine; orig. has simply "En portarse à la ocasion."

ccxci. *The care of the wise*, etc.—Orig. "Compita la atencion del juyzioso can la detencion del recatado."

ccxcv. From *El Discreto*, c. xix.

ccxcvi. *Noble qualities make noblemen*—Orig. "Las primeras hazen los primeros hombres."

ccc. *Three HHH's*—Orig. "Tres eses hazen dichoso, Santo, Sano y
Sabio." Schop. "Drei Dinge die in Spanischen mit einem S
anfangen machen glücklich —Heiligkeit, Gesundheit, and
Weisheit." M.G.D. "Three SSS render a man happy, Sanctity,
Soundness of body, and Sageness."

THE END

Made in the USA
Middletown, DE
20 March 2019